T0372792

Official Cambridge Exam Preparation ✓

OPEN WORLD

C1

ADVANCED

WORKBOOK

with answers
with Audio

Greg Archer

Cambridge University Press
www.cambridge.org/elt

Cambridge Assessment English
www.cambridgeenglish.org

Information on this title: www.cambridge.org/9781108891479

© Cambridge University Press & Assessment and UCLES 2021

First published 2021

20 19 18 17 16 15 14 13 12 11 10 9 8 7 6 5 4 3

Printed in Great Britain by CPI Group (UK) Ltd, Croydon CR0 4YY

A catalogue record for this publication is available from the British Library

ISBN   978-1-108-89147-9   Workbook with answers with Audio Download

CONTENTS

Material available online:

Answer Key and Audio scripts

TAKE IT FROM ME

GRAMMAR

1 **Read the article and answer the questions.**

1 Who decided to implement a new study skill?
2 Who learnt English to meet new acquaintances?
3 Who was greatly influenced by an unanticipated encounter?
4 Who was encouraged to learn for commercial reasons?
5 Who was initially reluctant to learn English?
6 Who felt upset about their lack of communication skills?

🏠 🔍   www.learningenglishblog.com   ← →

Saeed

I first ~~had~~ arrived here with my parents when I was eight. I was really worried about living in a new country, especially as I wasn't knowing the language at all. Not a word! I soon discovered that it had been impossible to make friends without being able to chat to them in any way, so I had been forcing myself to do it, even though I couldn't get my ideas across at all. But I made some amazing friends. Looking back, the best thing about it was how much they helped me – I had never regretted pushing myself out of my comfort zone.

Jules

By the time I left school, I was studying English for about six years, on and off, but not with any real interest. To tell you the truth, I looked forward to never saying another word in English. That summer, I went on holiday with my parents, and we had stayed in the same hotel as this Scottish family. The son, Nigel, was about my age. I never met anyone like him before, he was so open to adventure and had such a free spirit. I spent so much time talking to him about life, and what we both had hoped to get from it, I decided there and then to move to Scotland.

Johan

My parents were really wanting me to get better at English so I could become involved in their business. I registered for an online course and immediately was getting to work on my new language skills. Soon, my parents took me to a meeting with an Australian businessman who has been working with our company for several years. I couldn't understand a word, but knew immediately that I have been finding it so difficult to get what he was saying because I had never written anything down during my course, not a single word of vocabulary. I had improved since then, obviously!

2 **Find and correct five past verb form mistakes in each section of the article. The first one has been done for you.**

I first arrived here …

3 **Rearrange the words in bold to form correct sentences.**

1 There is little doubt that the city **busier / become / will / increasingly** over the next five years.

....

2 I **over / heading / to / hopefully / am** my sister's this evening.

....

3 What time should we meet? I think **starts / film / at / the / eight thirty**.

....

4 I'm afraid there are no places left, but **you / sure / stay / will / make / on / we** the waiting list.

....

5 The rain has been terrible all day, but I **far / to / is / going / it / worse / get / suspect** before it gets better.

....

6 For your party next week, **everyone / inviting / be / you / will** from work?

....

4 **Correct the mistakes in the sentences, then match them to the descriptions (A–E).**

1 I'd love to come to your party, but I'm not sure if I can. I'm letting you know tomorrow.
2 Markus says that he'll be here at five, unless the traffic is going to be dreadful.
3 Have you heard about that amazing new restaurant in town? We go at the weekend.
4 Suki will have her driving test at 11.00 tomorrow. That explains why she's so nervous.
5 I'm sure I make friends when I start college, but I still don't want to go.

A Expressing a future intention, desire, or promise.
B Making a prediction about the future.
C Using the present simple to describe a scheduled event at a known time in the future.
D Using the present simple in first conditional clauses after the condition or time word.
E Using the present continuous to talk about a fixed plan or arrangement.

VOCABULARY

Correct the spelling or word choice mistakes in the sentences. Tick (✔) any sentences which are correct.

1. Although we are so different, my best friend and I complement each other very well.
2. Ben was sitting among his parents when his university acceptance letter arrived.
3. I'd love to get some work experience at the gym, but I'm not sure whose the best person to contact.
4. I get nervous talking to the principle, but she always listens to what you're saying.
5. It's so much better when receipts are emailed to you – the paper ones are too easy to lose.
6. My school runs entirely on the principle that the harder you study, the better your grades.
7. My teacher told me I was the most opinionated student she had ever had. I took it as a complement.
8. Now that the rain has finally stopped, I'm feeling all together more optimistic than I was yesterday.
9. It doesn't matter whose fault it was, we need to make sure we fix this mess quickly.
10. That was a wonderful meal – the chef is fantastic! I'd love to get the receipt for my main course.
11. The wedding guests were gathered all together, waiting for the bride and groom to appear.
12. Walking through the countryside is among the most relaxing things anyone can do.

SPEAKING

1. Complete the dialogue with the correct options.

A I'm really enjoying our English lessons at the moment. The new teacher is really pushing us to improve with some of the activities we do, isn't she?

B (1) *Why's that? / Like what?*

A Well, getting us to use more idiomatic language in our speaking, for one thing. I feel like my conversations are starting to sound much more natural.

B (2) *That's true / I know what you mean.* I never realised how important that sort of thing is, if you're aiming to get to a really advanced level.

A (3) *No way! / Me neither.* I mean, when I started learning English, the teacher I had just made us do grammar exercises in every class. We never studied vocabulary and we certainly never practised our speaking.

B (4) *Really? / What a nightmare!*

A It was, but I just tried to keep reading as much as I could in English and kept a really good vocabulary notebook, even though the teacher never checked it.

B (5) *That sounds amazing, / That must have been frustrating,* especially because you were a student who really wanted to improve. My first teacher was nothing like that. In fact, every one of our classes was just focused on speaking.

A (6) *You're having me on! / You're so lucky!*

B Well, I'm not sure I'd say that. I don't think we learnt much vocabulary in his class, either. He certainly never got us to take notes. Anyway, at least we're both with a great teacher now.

A (7) *Exactly! / Me too!*

2. 🎧 02 **Listen and check your answers to Exercise 1.**

3. Complete the table with the words and phrases in italics from Exercise 1.

EXPRESSING AN EMOTIONAL RESPONSE	
EXPRESSING AGREEMENT/COMPREHENSION	
ASKING FOR MORE DETAIL	*Why's that?*

READING

1 Choose the correct heading for each of the sections (A–D).

1 The appeal of simplicity and accessibility
2 A victim of its own popularity
3 The more things change, the more they stay the same
4 Modern techniques are only useful in the right hands

A ....

Native speakers of English are today in the minority, outnumbered five to one by those who use it as a second, third or even fourth language. With this has come a number of changes in the way the language is spoken, as people from across the world come together to communicate as best they possibly can, even with low levels of ability. It has led to some interesting transformations. For example, we have seen the emergence of *Spanglish* and *Singlish*; English mixed with, respectively, Spanish and Singaporean, in many cases creating elements of an entirely new language. Additionally, huge numbers of traditional 'mistakes' in grammar or vocabulary have tended to be disregarded, becoming entirely acceptable in conversation, even 'correct'. For these reasons, some people believe that, a hundred years from now, English will have become completely unrecognisable from the way in which it is currently used.

B ....

Another school of thought is that although English will change, particularly as native speakers are no longer the dominant group, it is conceivable that on the whole it will probably remain fundamentally the same. For one thing, as mobile technology becomes increasingly popular worldwide, texting is having a huge effect on the way we 'talk' to one another. Far from being, as many critics argue, an excessive oversimplification of the language, all texting has actually done is provide people with another form in which to communicate. It helps to make some of the more involved aspects of English less difficult, yet at the same time allows for a huge range of expression and creativity. So, in the future, the *medium* of communication will undergo huge changes, not the language itself.

C ....

Globally, there is a growing proportion of people who have adopted English in addition to their own language, and this trend looks set to continue. A decade ago, it was expected that Chinese would soon replace English as the primary global language of communication, and a huge number of well-respected educators started encouraging schools to teach it to children from the age of four. Yet this development never quite happened and, in fact, some researchers now suggest that China is – or will soon become – the nation with the highest number of inhabitants who speak some form of English. Perhaps it is because the language is considered to be relatively easy to learn in comparison with most others spoken across the world. Indeed, given how easy it is to watch movies and TV shows in English, many people claim that they have learnt the language alone, in front of a screen. Equally importantly, though, most linguists believe that if you want to convey a simple message in simple terms, there is no better language available than English.

D ....

English is, for many, also the global language of business. There are hundreds of apps available which claim to provide a reliable, instantaneous translation service, and thus can help anyone who wants to become an international business executive, even if they have only a beginner level of English. But how effective are these apps for the businessperson of the future? In high-level meetings, where decisions often need to be made quickly and decisively, would it not seem unprofessional to frequently stop a discussion to translate something you want to say through an app on your phone? There is also a strong case to argue that translation apps, while indisputably useful for tourists, will always lack accuracy and reliability when it comes to business situations where exactness is key and misunderstanding should be avoided where possible. While there is no doubt that improvements in technology can help more people to communicate in English, it needs to be used wisely.

2 Which section in the text:

1 suggests that technology can be unreliable in certain situations? ....
2 disagrees with B about whether English will survive in the future? ....
3 mentions the idea that English benefits from its lack of complexity? ....
4 praises the flexibility that technology can bring to conversations? ....
5 describes a prediction that did not come true? ....

3 Find words or phrases in the text that mean:

1 ignored (para A) ....
2 believable (para B) ....
3 essentially (para B) ....
4 complicated (para B) ....
5 comparatively (para C) ....
6 deliver (para C) ....
7 immediate (para D) ....
8 unquestionably (para D) ....

LISTENING

1 🔊 03 Listen to Speakers A–C talking about their experiences of language learning. Which speaker mentions:

1 their intention to meet new people? ....
2 being able to resolve a frustrating situation? ....
3 making a sudden, unexpected decision? ....
4 sensing that a friendship has been improved because of their studies? ....
5 a lack of practice opportunities? ....
6 feeling a greater self-belief in their abilities? ....

2 🔊 03 Replace the underlined phrases in sentences 1–6 with the phrases in the box. Then listen again and check your answers.

| more often than not   really took off   out loud |
| word-perfect   immerse yourself in   tall order |

1 To be honest, making any sort of progress in either was a <u>real challenge</u>. ....
2 ... the more you understand of a language, the more you can relax and <u>integrate completely into</u> the local culture. ....
3 I find it really helps me to focus. Well, <u>most of the time</u>! ....
4 My language skills <u>improved very quickly</u> from the first class. ....
5 I was really anxious and thought I'd just freeze if I said it <u>so everyone else could hear</u>. ....
6 Not <u>100% correct</u>, but enough to get the point across. ....

WRITING

1 Complete the table with the pairs of matching formal and informal words and phrases in the box.

| ~~after all~~   a great number of   by way of example |
| entirely confused   far more demanding |
| far superior   huge influence   it's no great shock |
| it is little wonder   I mean   loads and loads of |
| massive effect   much harder   so much better |
| totally baffled   ~~ultimately~~ |

FORMAL	INFORMAL
ultimately	after all

2 Complete texts A and B with the correct words and phrases from the box.

Text A

Hi Antonio,

Good to hear from you, and thanks for asking how my Spanish lessons are going. If I'm being honest, a lot of the time I'm **(1)** .... about how to use all those verb forms correctly. **(2)** .... , in English, there aren't that many changes you can make to the form of a regular verb, but now I'm realising that there are **(3)** .... ways you need to transform a verb in Spanish if you want people to understand you properly. But **(4)** .... that I'm not making progress as quickly as I'd hoped. **(5)** .... , just the fact that I'm an adult makes things **(6)** .... I read this article the other day about how kids are **(7)** .... than older people at learning a second or third language. Apparently, as you age, your first language has a **(8)** .... on the way you learn another one, but kids don't have that. Maybe I'll just go into my next class and pretend I'm six!

Speak soon,

Colin

Text B

<u>The difficulties of language learning in 'teenagehood'</u>
In terms of learning a second or third language, the majority of research on the subject seems to prove that, **(1)** .... , children are **(2)** .... to teenagers in their ability to understand and absorb language in a way that they can produce it themselves.
Most teenagers find learning a language **(3)** .... than children do, and **(4)** .... that this is the case. **(5)** .... , while a regular verb in English might only be altered in four ways (e.g. *work, works, working, worked*), in Spanish there are **(6)** .... verb transformations that could occur if one wishes to be correctly understood. In this way, there is every reason for teenage students to find themselves **(7)** .... by the new ways in which verb forms are used in the language they are attempting to learn – at this point in their lives, they have already developed a full language system, and this tends to have a **(8)** .... on the learning process.

1 GOOD COMPANY

GRAMMAR

1 **Choose the correct option in each sentence.**

1   *Would/Could* you mind telling me about your extended family?

2   You may not get on with them now, but your parents are always going to be there for you, *aren't they/won't they*?

3   I was wondering *that you/if you* had Rayyan's number. I'd love to give him a call.

4   *Hadn't it been/Wouldn't it have been* a good idea to ask your dad before you took the car?

5   On *what/which* app did you meet your best online friend?

6   Life would be much easier without the constant pressure of social media, *weren't it/wouldn't it*?

2 **Match 1–8 with A–H and complete the sentences with the correct form of a verb in the box. The first one has been done for you.**

1   We should go out to celebrate *finishing our last year at school together. (E)*

2   Steve has had another row with his coach – he's threatened

3   I can't quite believe it, but my mum is letting me

4   Almost immediately, Tomas regretted

5   The more friends he made online, the less he could imagine ever

6   Maria's grandfather was getting old, so she never minded

7   The kids are only three, so there's no use

8   After ten years apart, she was delighted

| enjoy | ~~finish~~ | go | hear | help | leave | send | take |

A   the team.

B   life with real people again.

C   about what he had done since they last met.

D   that angry text to his brother.

E   ~~our last year at school together.~~

F   to the concert on Saturday on my own.

G   them to the cinema for a few years yet.

H   him out with his shopping.

VOCABULARY

1 🔊 04 **Listen to five people describing someone they know. Choose the correct adjective that describes the person they are talking about. Then write the noun form of each adjective.**

| restless | selfish | humble | conscientious | narrow-minded |

1   adjective .... noun ....
2   adjective .... noun ....
3   adjective .... noun ....
4   adjective .... noun ....
5   adjective .... noun ....

2 **Put the adjectives in the box into the table to make the correct negative forms.**

| ~~approachable~~ | biased | competent | flexible | likeable | loyal | obedient |
| passionate | patient | polite | prejudiced | rational | responsible | sincere | tolerant |

UN-	IN-	DIS-	IM-	IR-
approachable				

3 **Correct the mistakes with prefixes in the adjectives.**

1   I don't know why Mariam still goes to French class with that imcompetent teacher – I learnt nothing in the six weeks I attended the course.

2   My sister has a totally inrational fear of rabbits – they're not scary at all!

3   My dog Fido has been really unobedient lately, so I'm going to take him to puppy training classes.

4   In your completely disbiased opinion, is my essay for Professor Smith too critical?

5   It was so inresponsible of you and Mo to go to that party the night before your exam.

6   I need help with my art project, but the teacher is rather irapproachable.

PUSH YOURSELF C2

Correct the mistakes in the relationship idioms.

1   My flatmate always eats my food without asking and **to put injury on insult,** he never bothers to replace it.

2   My sister and I are identical twins, but we're **poles away** when it comes to personality.

3   You need to watch what you say around Marco at the moment. He's **got a few chips on his shoulder** after he didn't get the promotion.

4   My cousins are all great. I've always **got on with them like a home in a fire**.

5   I'd love to come out tonight, but I'm **in my parents' naughty books** after I failed that exam.

6   My sister posted a nasty comment on a photo I shared – I was **reduced to crying**.

You are going to read an article about making friends online. For questions 1–6, choose the answer (A, B, C or D) which you think fits best according to the text.

Fair-weather friends for hire

'So, how did you two meet?' In today's world, such an enquiry is likely to be met with a familiar, one-word response: 'online'. Indeed, according to latest figures, for modern city dwellers, there is now a 30% chance that the couple will have met online. By 2050, this figure may even have doubled. What makes this development even more intriguing is the fact that only fifty years ago, to the population of the self-same city, its whole concept would have seemed unequivocally alien, as people typically met their partners through friends or family connections. Today, however, there is a universal acceptance that romantic attachments can, and very often do, begin online.

line 8

Friendships, though, are apparently another matter, with people still typically preferring real world encounters to their virtual equivalents. But this could all be about to change. Into the supposed void have stepped a small-but-growing band of entrepreneurs such as Karl Dunning, founder of *Rentapal*. These people have established websites which they claim offer a uniquely contemporary service: for a specified time period, members can hire someone to pose as their friend. It is an already established industry in Japan, one which Dunning, amongst others, saw as ripe for worldwide expansion, and with a self-consciously noble philosophy at its core. "It's not about making money – I want to alleviate the pain of hidden loneliness that runs through our world today".

Just as dating websites allow users to fine-tune their complex preferences, *Rentapal* provides members with a tried-and-tested array of filter options, such as personality type, age, and so on, in their quest to find non-romantic companionship. Should you need a local guide during your stay in a new city, Dunning's site can match you with someone appropriate. Has your gym partner suddenly suffered an injury, leaving you with no one to chat to? At the click of a button, you can work through various options to find yourself an appropriate companion. Simply pay a membership fee, then another for your new friend's time, plus any expenses required for their session with you.

Maude (not her real name) works as a *Rentapal* 'friend'. She talks enthusiastically about the adventures and opportunities that come her way through the site, seeing herself not simply as a paid companion, but also as a quasi-therapist. "Most clients just need someone to talk to. I'm there to listen, to empathise, and provide much-needed reassurance." On the surface, then, this is a faultless service. And yet, while Dunning rhapsodises about the long-term friendships that have supposedly been built thanks to his website, the overarching snag, as Maude coldly explains, is that many of the people who engage her services immediately come to see her as a genuine friend after the first meeting. At which point, "since they don't want to pay me for any more of my time, I stop seeing them, however much I might enjoy their company".

Dunning, though, passionately believes in his mission to bring people together. He argues that "if we dedicated half as much time as we do to staring at our smartphones, and instead took a moment to look up and talk to the person next to us on the bus," such solitude would eventually disappear from society. As convincing as this argument undoubtedly is, he overlooks the obvious irony that engaging the services of his website requires the very screen time he so stridently criticises. Yet, despite his somewhat ill-conceived argument, loneliness is indeed very much on the rise in societies the world over. A huge study undertaken recently in the US suggested that, using the renowned UCLA Loneliness Scale, over half of Americans consider themselves to be lonely.

Dunning is adamant that true, lasting friendships have come out of his *Rentapal* matchmaking, and is currently working on a way to track the success stories, much in the same way as dating websites do for successful pairings. Maude, however, is less convinced that we are at the dawn of dynamic change in our social interaction. Their views may never be reconciled because, at the root of the matter, it is all so difficult to pin down. However accustomed as we now are to the idea of paying for a series of expensive blind dates that lead absolutely nowhere, we still feel far more prickly and awkward when we are asked to invest monetarily in a potential friendship, particularly if it is so one-sided.

1 In line 8, what does the word *its* refer to?

A city   **C** population
B fact   **D** development

2 In the second paragraph, what does the writer suggest about friendship websites?

A They could only have been invented recently.
B They address a problem that might not necessarily exist.
C They are set up according to a strict set of principles.
D They are essentially profit-motivated.

3 In the third paragraph, what point does the writer make about *Rentapal*?

A It is a cost-effective way to make friends.
B It is mainly aimed at tourists.
C It is too complicated for the average user.
D It is conventional in its design.

4 What does the writer suggest about Maude in the fourth paragraph?

A She is a trained psychiatrist.
B She has a thrill-seeking personality.
C She prioritises finance over friendship.
D She is reluctant to meet clients more than once.

5 In the fifth paragraph, it is clear that the writer

A admires Dunning's passion for his business.
B disagrees with Dunning's reasoning about smartphones.
C enjoys Dunning's manner of speaking.
D believes that Dunning's argument is inconsistent.

6 What is the writer's view about the nature of friendships formed through the website?

A It is reasonable to describe it in financial terms.
B It is likely to undergo significant change in the near future.
C It is sometimes the foundation of a successful marriage.
D It is resistant to any concrete definition.

SPEAKING PART 1

1 Which of the following questions would the examiner *not* ask in Speaking Part 1? Why not?

A How important is it for you to spend time with your friends?
B What can people do to keep in touch with friends or family more easily?
C What do you most often use social media for?
D Who is the tallest person in your family?
E Do you feel happier being with a small or a large group of friends?
F Why might someone move very far away from their family and friends?

2 🌐 05 Listen to three exam candidates. Which of the questions (A–F) are they answering?

Candidate 1: Question _____   Candidate 2: Question _____   Candidate 3: Question _____

3 🌐 05 Listen to the candidates again. Put a tick or a cross in the table next to the questions.

DO THE CANDIDATES ...	CANDIDATE 1	CANDIDATE 2	CANDIDATE 3
correctly respond to the question being asked?			
use higher level vocabulary/grammar?			
produce an answer of an appropriate length for Part 1?			

4 🌐 06 Listen to candidates 2 and 3 again. Which advanced-level language do they use to mean the following?

1 It depends where I am _____
2 I'm not outgoing and sociable with everyone _____
3 a busy party place full of lots of good friends _____
4 I use it too much, like everyone else _____
5 Many people dislike it _____
6 I don't really agree with that _____

2 ON THE MOVE

1 Choose the correct option in each sentence. There may be more than one correct answer.

1 *Simply/Sadly/Frankly*, I won't be able to come and visit you this weekend. Unfortunately I just missed the last train.

2 *On the whole/As a whole/Wholly*, I find the process of flying to another country really exciting, despite all the waiting around you have to do.

3 *Frequently/Typically/Uncharacteristically*, it's difficult to travel across town at peak times.

4 *Unsurprisingly/Fortunately/Regrettably*, they let me take my suitcase on as hand luggage, so when we landed I could bypass baggage reclaim and head straight for the exit.

5 You don't need to take a jacket as you'll only be outside for a moment. *Beside/Besides/Nevertheless*, it's going to be 30 degrees and sunny when we land.

6 *Surely/Predictably/Unquestionably*, given the amount of money that has been spent on upgrading the network, there shouldn't be any more long delays on the Metro.

2 Complete the sentences with the correct word or phrase in the box. There are six words or phrases that you do not need.

| The whole | a little | both | another | none | others |
| much | together | little | plenty | All | neither |

1 When we were travelling, we were grateful for any help we got, however _____ that was.

2 There are _____ of us who would be happy to pay more tax on fuel, as long as it was genuinely reinvested in the right ways.

3 For each person who prefers travelling by train, there is _____ who simply cannot leave their car at home.

4 _____ time we were in Thailand I only called my parents twice. I didn't realise how worried they were.

5 I was quite annoyed when the 12.20 bus didn't arrive. I waited for the 12.50 service, but in the end _____ of them turned up, so I was late!

6 After finally touching down safely, the pilots _____ agreed that it had been the most difficult landing of their careers.

VOCABULARY

1 Complete sentences a and b with the same word from the box.

diversion	track	board	reversed	wreck

1 **a** Our train's been delayed. Apparently it's due to a problem with the _____ , but that's what they always say.

    b Your driving instructor will make every effort to _____ your progress and give feedback after each lesson.

2 **a** Oh no! I've just _____ the car into the neighbour's fence and I think he saw me do it!

    b Why on earth has the government _____ its decision to invest in electric car technology?

3 **a** The police couldn't believe that the motorbike wasn't a complete _____ after the accident.

    b Unless you start saving soon, you'll _____ your chances of going travelling next year.

4 **a** The traffic jam was caused by the _____ around the roadworks in the city centre.

    b My main _____ from boredom on the plane was reading the in-flight magazine.

5 **a** There have been improvements across the _____ in journey times since the new bus lane opened.

    b Sorry, I can't talk now, I'm already on _____ the plane. I'll call you when I land.

2 Complete the text with the option (A–D) that best fits each gap.

When my dad first suggested I train to be a driving instructor, I was in two **(1)** _____ about it. **(2)** _____, I'd just retired from professional car racing and was desperate to get back on **(3)** _____ again. The idea of becoming an instructor was quite appealing for different reasons. **(4)** _____ a start, I loved working with cars, and the job was perfect for me in **(5)** _____ of my knowledge of advanced driving techniques. Anyway, I signed up for a course and got myself up to **(6)** _____ with the teaching side of the job. To **(7)** _____ extent, it feels like this was a natural transition from racing. As they say, those who can, do; those who can't, teach!

1	**A**	ideas	**C**	reasons
	B	minds	**D**	thoughts
2	**A**	At times	**C**	That time
	B	At the time	**D**	All the time
3	**A**	route	**C**	roads
	B	the street	**D**	the road
4	**A**	If	**C**	For
	B	To	**D**	By
5	**A**	terms	**C**	facts
	B	ways	**D**	sense
6	**A**	pace	**C**	speed
	B	tempo	**D**	measure
7	**A**	that	**C**	this
	B	some	**D**	any

PUSH YOURSELF C2

Complete each sentence with a prepositional phrase from the box. There is one phrase that you do not need.

at the best of times	by way of apology for
in favour of	in retrospect	in the vicinity of
on impulse	out of season

"The airline refunded my ticket **(1)** _____ the ridiculously long delay, which was somewhere **(2)** _____ eight hours, in the end. I'm not a very patient person **(3)** _____ , but this was unbearable, especially since we were flying **(4)** _____ . There was hardly anyone else in the airport! **(5)** _____ , I should never have expected much – the flight company has only got a one-star rating online, but I saw the low price and bought the flight **(6)** _____ . I won't be doing that again!"

07 You will hear an interview in which two students called Susie Ward and Tom Smith are talking about their travel experiences.

For questions 1–6, choose the answer (A, B, C or D) which fits best according to what you hear.

1 What does Susie say was the main reason for their decision to go travelling?
- **A** They wanted to gain valuable work experience abroad.
- **B** They needed to prove to themselves that they could do it.
- **C** They wanted to maintain a certain aspect of their current lives.
- **D** They needed to take a complete break during their studies.

2 How did Susie feel after they had asked around for guidance?
- **A** inspired to go travelling immediately
- **B** rewarded by their use of an appropriate tone
- **C** disappointed in their friends' suggestions
- **D** surprised by how many people were willing to help

3 Tom explains that, during the early stages of their travels, he and Susie
- **A** were excessively naïve in their feelings about the trip.
- **B** were forced by circumstances to change their itinerary.
- **C** were struggling to cope with the constant exhaustion.
- **D** were finding the lack of social contact difficult.

4 What point does Tom make when he tells the story about the sunset?
- **A** Travellers should always prioritise their appreciation of nature.
- **B** Travelling is impossible when visiting places without internet access.
- **C** Travellers usually rely on the kindness of strangers.
- **D** Luck and chance encounters can make travelling easier.

5 What advice would Susie give as a result of her travels?
- **A** Don't organise things too far ahead.
- **B** Don't be tempted to get rid of necessary items.
- **C** Make sure you set off with an open mind.
- **D** Always keep your emotions under control.

6 Susie and Tom agree that they are both especially proud of
- **A** their ability to cope with rejection.
- **B** their work with less privileged people.
- **C** their capacity for inventiveness.
- **D** their gift for interpersonal communication.

WRITING PART 1: ESSAY

1 Read the Writing Part 1 task and the sample essay. Find 11 mistakes that match the descriptions (A–K). Write the number of the line where the mistake appears.

> Your class has attended a discussion about how going travelling is good for young people's personal development. You have made the notes below:
>
> Ways that travelling can benefit young people:
> - self-confidence
> - experience of new culture(s)
> - gain new friends
>
> Some opinions expressed in the discussion:
>
> "You become more independent and assured in your ideas."
>
> "Experiencing other cultures broadens your horizons."
>
> "Travelling helps you to meet people like yourself."
>
> Write an essay discussing two of the ways in your notes that travelling can benefit young people. You should explain which way you think is more effective, giving reasons to support your opinion.
>
> You may, if you wish, make use of the opinions expressed in the discussion, but you should use your own words as far as possible.

2 Write the corrections to Exercise 1 in the gaps below.

A ....*their*.......................
B ....
C ....
D ....
E ....
F ....
G ....
H ....
I ....
J ....
K ....

3 Which is the best conclusion for the essay, Paragraph A or B?

A With the above in mind, I would argue that the most important benefit of travelling is in living among new people in fresh environments. It is, in fact, the source of all other positive opportunities and outcomes that emerge from such exploration of the world.

B The final point is that any traveller is likely to come across like-minded people, some of whom are very likely to become good friends for life. Each and every one of the three benefits is of importance, I would argue.

1	For many years, young people <u>are using</u> travel as a way to experience life from new angles.
2	By doing so, not only do they become more self-assured, but they can also develop their
3	<u>social skill</u>.
4	In many cases, going travelling presents them with their <u>first opportunity spending</u> a long
5	period of time away from their families. Living at home with <u>their parents young people</u> may
6	become a little overprotected, and often do not need to think for themselves, particularly in
7	terms of understanding their place in the world. Spending long periods of time <u>outside of</u>
8	comfort zones and questioning <u>a</u> life they have led up to that point can greatly encourage them
9	to become more mature and gain confidence in their views.
10	Further to this, encountering new people and sights in <u>cultural unfamiliar contexts</u> can greatly
11	influence anybody, but especially those who are at an <u>impresionable</u> age when their minds are
12	<u>considerably open</u> to new adventures. While it is fair to say that the world, thanks to
13	technological innovations, <u>have become</u> a smaller place than ever in so many ways, there is no
14	doubt that first-hand experience in life is <u>to</u> the utmost importance. Societies differ from city to
15	city, and even more so from country to country, so it should be impossible for travellers not to
16	be influenced by what and whom they come into contact with.

A missing word ....7.......
B incorrect tense used ....
C wrong article ....
D wrong preposition used ....
E error with word order ....
F singular used instead of plural ....
G wrong adverb used before adjective ....
H spelling mistake with single/double letter ....
I subject/verb agreement ....
J error with use of infinitive/gerund ....
K missing punctuation ....

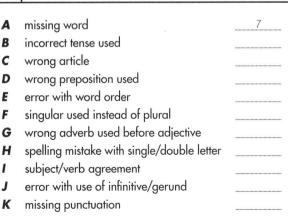
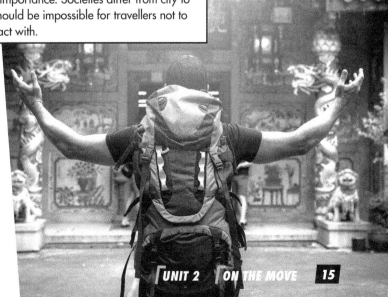

3 ROLLING IN MONEY

GRAMMAR

1 Tick (✔) the correct sentences. Correct those which contain an error.

1 If you need any help in choosing the right bank account, please don't hesitate to ask myself.

2 In any successful corporation, it is vital that managers communicate with the other.

3 Since January, I've been applying myself for about three jobs per week, but every single one so far has turned me down.

4 Rahul was pleasantly surprised when they him offered retirement, five years early.

5 Arianna was so proud when her teacher recommended her for the Business Studies course.

6 After closing the deal, Tobias knew that his boss would finally give him the credit he deserved.

7 My business doesn't run itself, so for me being self-employed means that I can never completely switch me off and relax.

8 Guille and Paco are always in competition with each one another to see who can spend their week's wages the quickest.

2 Complete the conditional sentences with the options in the box. Use each option once only.

as soon as	in case	otherwise
provided	supposing	unless

1 I'll happily hand over my money, _____ you tell me how exactly you're planning to invest it.

2 _____ I gave up working full time, would we have enough money to pay the bills?

3 I think we should offer the job to Helene, _____ you've got other ideas?

4 _____ you were wondering, it costs almost £500 to stay in that hotel per night.

5 Anyone can have a financially secure retirement, _____ you start saving early enough.

6 My company really should start investing in its staff, _____ people will start leaving soon.

3 Complete the conditional sentences with the correct form of the verbs in brackets. Use the positive (+) or negative (-) form of the verbs as indicated.

1 Where would we _____ now if money _____? (be (+) / invent (-))

2 Anyone can _____ themselves into a success if they _____ hard enough. (turn (+) / work (+))

3 I'd never _____ to working for my parents, even if they _____ me a six-figure salary. (go back (+) / offer (+))

4 If you _____ to keep the paperwork in order, we _____ that several payments were overdue. (neglect (-) / notice (+))

5 Assuming that your business targets _____ overly ambitious, we _____ keen to invest. (be (-) / be (+))

6 I'm afraid I definitely _____ you at the conference unless my boss _____ me take that day off. (see (-) / let (+))

1 Complete the extracts from the autobiography of businesswoman Julianna Beruhaza with the words in the box below.

| affluent | assets | bankruptcy | break even | expenditure | lucrative | overdraft | prosperity | rip-off | squander |

I certainly didn't expect to make any sort of profit from my first year of trading, but I still managed to **(1)** _____ , which is extremely rare for a business start-up. This is partly because I kept such a close watch over the two fundamental pillars of running a business – income and **(2)** _____ . Plus, I had managed to negotiate a considerable **(3)** _____ with the bank, which allowed me to operate with greater financial freedom than I would have otherwise.

It has always been easy for me to identify what is a good deal, and what is a **(4)** _____ . If you want to be successful, if you want to be extremely **(5)** _____ , whatever you do, do not **(6)** _____ money on risky investments. They may look like more **(7)** _____ options, as high levels of risk bring greater profit, but this is a fool's game.

I also knew from day one that, although **(8)** _____ does not mean the end of your business career, it should only ever be a last resort. Too many people now see it as a way to clear their debts and start again, but your reputation will suffer greatly. I also realised that it was madness to keep hold of your **(9)** _____ for too long – your car, for example, goes down in value every time you drive it.

Work all the hours that you possibly can, including weekends. The only time I was able to relax was the moment I decided I could finally retire and live in great **(10)** _____ if I wanted to. And yet, despite that, you'll still find me in the office at 7 a.m. every day!

2 Complete the second sentence so that it has a similar meaning to the first sentence, using the word given. Do not change the word given. Use between three and six words.

1 During the first day in his new job, Chris immediately made friends with the office gossip.
TIME
During the first day in his new job, Chris _____ friends with the office gossip.

2 I used to work as a salesperson.
LIVING
I used to _____ as a salesperson.

3 You can't leave home until you have no further debts to pay.
BEEN
You can't leave home until your debts _____ in full.

4 Apparently, many billionaires donate money to charity purely to avoid paying tax.
MAKE
Many billionaires are _____ to charity purely to avoid paying tax.

5 I borrowed some money from my friend and forgot to repay him.
BACK
I forgot about _____ after he lent me some money.

6 If each part of the course is paid for separately, you may find it easier to manage your finances.
INSTALMENTS
Should you _____ , you may find it easier to manage your finances.

Correct the mistakes in the money idioms.

1 New government figures show that the number of people **living mouth to mouth** has increased by 2% in the last 12 months.

2 After receiving her inheritance, she decided to pay off her credit card and **splash out for** a new car.

3 My rent has increased so much that I am finding it hard **to make costs meet** every month.

4 Spending an extra £5 per month on food is certainly not going to **break my wallet**.

5 If we are going to be able to afford an overseas holiday this year, we are going to need to **tighten our trousers**.

6 For the first time since I left university, my bank account isn't **on the red** and I am able to save for a house deposit.

7 I'd love to buy a house closer to the centre, but they **cost the planet**, so I am looking in the suburbs.

8 Personal finances should be taught in all schools so that young people learn to **live inside their means**.

For questions **1–8**, read the text below. Use the word given in capitals at the end of some of the lines to form a word that fits in the gap **in the same line**. There is an example at the beginning (0).

Write your answers **IN CAPITAL LETTERS**.

| ANSWER: | (0) | P | R | E | D | I | C | T | A | B | L | Y |

The Life of an Entrepreneur

Many people decide early on that following a career path that is **(0)** .... mundane is not for them. Instead, the life of an entrepreneur is **(1)** .... appealing, despite the long working hours and having to deal with the **(2)** .... setbacks that they inevitably come up against on a regular basis. What happens when a business venture results in an **(3)** .... that they were not expecting, or if their latest project fails? The simple fact is, there is often a **(4)** .... familiar price to pay for being an entrepreneur. The long hours, the stress and the constant pressure that comes from being **(5)** .... all take their toll. This worry usually leads to long nights of uncomfortable **(6)** .... , and feeling exhausted has never helped anyone to close that next deal. Ultimately, great consideration needs to be taken when deciding on the **(7)** .... of a steady job in favour of a tempting, but ultimately more **(8)** .... working life.

PREDICT
WHOLE

COUNT
COME

DEPRESS
WORK

SLEEP

ABANDON
TEST

1 ⓐ 08 **Listen to two students discussing the question, "Which factors might influence people's choice in how they spend their money?" Match the extracts to the following factors they discuss.**

friends _____   advertising _____   location _____

2 ⓐ 08 **Listen again and complete the gaps in the conversation.**

1 **A:** It's always going to form a big part of what people want and what they might aspire to, isn't it?
  B: _____ ?

2 **A:** …to be part of a crowd, **if you know** _____ **at**.
  B: Possibly. **If I've** _____ **here**, you're suggesting that …

3 **B:** …or just enjoy spending time with.
  A: _____ .
  B: Okay, **I might** _____ **on that, though** …

4 **A:** …for the same price elsewhere.
  B: _____ **if** _____ .

5 **A:** Go into town, on the other hand…
  B: Ah, so _____ **if** _____ , but …

6 **B:** …at that point in time.
  A: _____ .
  B: Okay, _____ **point,** but …

7 **B:** So, if I'm not mistaken, what you're saying is that we have no choice but to give in to suggestion?
  A: _____ .
  B: To be honest, _____ **I'd** _____ **that** …

3 **Complete the table with the phrases you completed in Exercise 2.**

CHECKING UNDERSTANDING	QUESTIONING A VIEWPOINT	CONFIRMING UNDERSTANDING	INTRODUCING A CONTRASTING OPINION

4 THE NATURAL WORLD

GRAMMAR

1 Complete the sentences with the correct form of the verb. The number of words needed is given.

1 By the time you go to bed tonight, another 200,000 acres of rainforest will
_____
(destroy, three words)

2 Tomorrow morning, the government is _____ the details of its plans to invest in renewable energy. (announce, two words)

3 Apart from taking a short break in June, the underwater exploration team will
_____
their work for the entire year. (continue, two words)

4 Hopefully, before long, every one of us will _____
that a plant-based diet is the only way forward. (realise, two words)

5 At some point in the future, Earth's entire population may well
_____ to other planets. (relocate, two words)

6 When the shuttle eventually begins its journey back to Earth, the astronauts will
_____ in space for almost two years. (live, three words)

7 Huge changes to our lifestyles are imperative if there
_____ any hope of saving the planet from further environmental damage. (be, three words)

2 Complete each sentence with the correct form of a multi-word verb from the box. Use each verb twice.

back up	call on	clear up	kill off	put aside

1 Once they had _____ their differences, the council leaders agreed on a set of measures to work towards a clean air policy.

2 Today, we _____ international organisations to start working together more effectively to address climate change.

3 The Space Agency is hoping its investigation into the shuttle crash will _____ any remaining questions once and for all.

4 Corinna _____ her claims about the future of driverless cars by giving a fantastic speech at the conference.

5 Many strains of bacteria can be effectively _____ by appropriate use of antibiotics.

6 Elephants are able to _____ their astonishing memories to follow the same migratory routes every year.

7 I always make sure to _____ some money each month to offset my carbon footprint.

8 Hearing about the negative impacts of tourism on Lan Hoi Island has completely _____ my desire to visit.

9 Every rush hour the traffic gets _____ from the ring road to the city centre. No wonder the air quality is so awful here.

10 Don't worry if the beach looks misty and wet now. Apparently it's going to _____ later.

3 Which sentences in Exercise 2 could be rewritten with the main verb and particle split?

1 *Once they had put their differences aside …*

VOCABULARY

1 Complete the crossword puzzle. Use the clues to help you. All the answers are words/phrases connected to space.

Across

3 It is thought the dinosaurs became extinct after an _____ crashed into the Earth.

4 Saturn's moon, Titan, is the only _____ in our Solar System with an atmosphere.

6 I had an amazing time in Japan. The food was on another _____ .

7 I'll take the stairs, you can have the lift to yourself. I get really nervous in _____ (two words).

9 I can't wait for _____ to become commonplace. I'd love to visit the moon (two words).

10 I need a new laptop. The _____ doesn't work on mine, I can only type one long word! (two words)

Down

1 We should get the earlier train. It'll give us some _____ and make sure we don't end up rushing to make the connection (two words).

2 Petrol is getting so expensive because the price of oil has gone into _____ this year.

5 Our tour guide was a total _____ – didn't seem to have a clue what he was talking about (three words).

8 Sixty years ago, the idea of going abroad on holiday every year was completely _____ to most people.

2 Correct the noun collocation errors in the review. Tick (✔) any which are correct.

Home | More reviews... | TV guide

A World of Regret, CBC's latest series on **(1) climate change**, is without question utterly **(2) impulsive viewing**. We begin the first episode flying alongside a golden eagle, that majestic **(3) bird of attack,** as it soars through its **(4) natural habitat** in a desperate search for sustenance. Not only is every detail of its increasingly precarious existence at the top of the **(5) food chain** shown in razor-sharp detail, but the rocky ridge of the **(6) mountain series** hundreds of metres below adds a backdrop of great beauty; this is cinematography at its finest. In another **(7) memorable scene** from a later episode, you can't help but admire the camera crews, battling against the **(8) ocean currents** in their quest to film one of the most majestic **(9) naval mammals** of all, the blue whale. Following its epic journey across the Pacific, the narrator gives a detailed account of the overwhelming **(10) assortment of species** that live beneath the waves. For each creature that comes into focus, we learn about the difficulties increasingly faced by almost every organism on our planet.

In addition to this, the producers have added a twist to the traditional nature show format by choosing to include contributions from the **(11) planet famous** scientist, Sandrine von Trapp. A **(12) central figure** in environmental activism, she puts across a **(13) compulsive case** for immediate action to halt the potential devastation that awaits us in the future; the horrifying results of over-exploitation of **(14) fossil energies**.

PUSH YOURSELF C2

Complete the sentences with the correct form of the verb *feel* + *anxious*, *optimistic* or *relieved*.

1 I know your brother really didn't want to get a malaria vaccine but, after he got bitten by that mosquito, I'm pretty sure he will _____ that he had.

2 All of you, I'd imagine, will _____ that there hasn't been any news about the space mission. All we can tell you is, at this time, they have not yet reached Mars.

3 Due to the success of recent flight tests, engineers will _____ about the new drones for a while now.

09 You will hear five short extracts in which people talk about changes they have made to benefit the environment.

TASK ONE

For questions 1–5, choose from the list (A–H) each speaker's main reason for becoming more environmentally friendly.

A   to improve physical well-being
B   to meet a long-term ethical objective
C   to encourage others to act in a similar way
D   to fulfil their new-found sense of responsibility
E   to impress a former friend
F   to personally object to a common practice in society
G   to cut down on household bills
H   to exploit a change in circumstances

Speaker 1   1 ....
Speaker 2   2 ....
Speaker 3   3 ....
Speaker 4   4 ....
Speaker 5   5 ....

TASK TWO

For questions 6–10, choose from the list (A–H) what each speaker has found most difficult about the decision they have made.

A   adjusting to different seasons
B   buying eco-friendly food
C   being reminded of past behaviour
D   sticking to a change in habits
E   satisfying the wishes of loved ones
F   coping with physical demands
G   feeling unsupported by acquaintances
H   balancing daily priorities

Speaker 1   6 ....
Speaker 2   7 ....
Speaker 3   8 ....
Speaker 4   9 ....
Speaker 5   10 ....

You have just completed a week's work experience in a travel company which helps visitors best enjoy the area where you live. The company director has asked you to write a report. In your report, you should describe what regions the visitors most and least enjoyed, what you did to make their stay more comfortable, and how the travel package could be improved in the future.

Write your **report**.

●●● ↶ ↻   🖫 🏠

Introduction

This report is intended to provide information about the regions clients visited, what they appreciated about the area and how we made their stay more comfortable. At the same time, potential improvements to services will be suggested.

Regions

(A) Many, in fact, stated that they wouldn't have come at all, had they known that this region would form a part of the tour. **(B)** The former failed to impress many of our visitors, over a quarter of whom complained about the lack of beauty in the area. **(C)** During the time I spent with the company, our clients were able to explore many of the more popular natural attractions of the area, starting with the Alabaster Flats and finishing with an overnight stay on the beaches near Bintanbrook. **(D)** Bintanbrook, on the other hand, demonstrated its typical seasonal weather, and the ensuing storms and rainbows captivated the onlookers completely.

Accommodation

All visitors **(1) had took** advantage of an odd situation at the four-star Bintan Hotel. After some initial **(2) clarity** _____ about where our clients were staying, during which time they were taken to, but then immediately removed from, the rooms they had been **(3) distributed** _____ , we registered a **(4) compliment** _____ to the hotel manager and managed to **(5) bargain** _____ an upgrade for everyone. As a result, every one of our guests was **(6) frustrated** _____ to be staying in a suite.

Recommendations

If I organised any subsequent trips, I would suggest the following:
* requested / avoided / should / Alabaster Flats / be / a client / to / Unless / by / a visit

1 _____

* visits / providing / weather / appeal / Bintanbrook / great / during / stormy / occur / holds

2 _____

* Bintan Hotel / should / partnerships / made / be / Future / the / with

3 _____

1 Read the Writing Part 2: Report task. Reorder the four sentences in the *Regions* section to create a logical paragraph (A–D).

2 Replace the words in bold in the *Accommodation* section with the correct form of the words in the box. An example has been done for you.

allocate	complain	confuse
delight	negotiate	~~take~~

3 Re-order the words in the *Recommendations* section to create correct sentences. Punctuate the sentences as needed.

5 SURFING, SCROLLING AND SWIPING

GRAMMAR

1 Tick (✔) the sentences where both underlined words/phrases are possible.

1 I'm sorry, but we <u>needn't/are under no obligation to</u> repair your laptop for free after the warranty has expired.

2 Somewhere on the internet there <u>must/has to</u> be an app that can do my Chemistry homework for me.

3 There's a rumour going around that YouTube are going to make every video 'paid-for', but <u>there's no way that's/it can't be</u> true, surely?

4 5G mobile internet is phenomenal. It <u>allows you to/has the ability of</u> download a movie in under a minute.

5 If you want to watch next week's webinar on creative game design, <u>you should/it is imperative to</u> register your interest early.

6 On this course, <u>it is mandatory/it is vital</u> for students to have a solid understanding of HTML-coding by the time they graduate.

7 What makes fingerprint login so practical is <u>not having to/not being obligated to</u> type in your password each time you unlock your phone.

2 In which ticked sentences in Exercise 1 do the options have a similar meaning?

3 Correct the relative pronouns and clauses in bold in each sentence.

1 At present, our new software can only be operated by 'Super-users', **by that** I mean those who have special permission to use it.

2 The technology in our college is pretty unreliable, particularly the Wi-Fi and the air con, **neither of them** ever seem to work properly.

3 Please name the website **what** impact has, in your eyes, been the biggest across the world.

4 Plans to sell commercial space flights have been criticised by experts, **much of whom** believe that the project is doomed to failure.

5 There has been widespread outrage regarding the government's new Internet Tax Plan, **to which** the public were never consulted.

6 The school **which** Bill Gates and Paul Allen first met is to be recognised as a 'Place of National Interest' by the US Government.

VOCABULARY

1 Replace the words in bold with the correct word from the box. You may have to change the form of the word.

boost	deteriorate	facilitate
hinder	~~outnumber~~	weaken

1 As of this year, cryptocurrencies by far **hinder**
outnumber their traditional equivalents by
around nine to one.

2 Our National Security Agency has been
progressively **boosted** by the relentless
cyberattacks on its infrastructure.

3 The latest innovation in AI technology has brought
with it a welcome **facilitation** for tech investors.

4 Juan was determined that nothing would
deteriorate his chances of becoming the next
Silicon Valley billionaire.

5 Online fraud is **upgraded** by people using the
same password for every account.

6 Smartphone batteries tend to **weaken**
alarmingly in their third year of use.

PUSH YOURSELF C2

Match the sentences (1–5) to the sentences with the
correct phrase with *dare* (A–E).

1 I'm going to tell Dad that you broke his laptop.

2 You've just got an email from your tutor – maybe it's
your exam result!

3 I've just reached 20,000 followers! Everyone loves
my latest posts!

4 Apparently, you're absolutely awful at online games.

5 Look! The teacher has left his computer unlocked.

A And I dare say that we won't hear the end of it for
a while.

B How dare you, I'm top of the leader board!

C Don't you dare!

D I dare you to put a fake post up on his Facebook
page.

E I daren't look.

2 Complete Alan's advice to his grandparents, who have
just bought their first computer, with the correct form of
the words in the box.

back up	hack into	log on	lock out
print out	strengthen	type in	

Hi Gran and Grandad!
I'm so happy you've bought a computer! Let me see if I can
give you some tips.
Sometimes you may find that you have forgotten
your password and can't **(1)** ....
to your account. Whatever you do, don't keep
(2) .... different passwords again
and again – you'll get **(3)** .... of
your account.
Change your password regularly (you can
(4) .... it by using a combination of
letters and characters, e.g. '!') The last thing you want is
for cyber criminals to **(5)** .... your
computer and access your bank accounts.
One thing I can't emphasise enough is to make sure you
(6) .... your files. That doesn't mean
(7) .... everything and keeping it in a
file on a shelf. I'll show you what you need to do to save
things on your computer.
Hope that helps!
Love, Alan

You are going to read an article about podcasts. For questions 1–10, choose from the sections (A–D). The sections may be chosen more than once.

In Praise of the Podcast

A

Back in the 1990s, pioneers of the podcast found that their time was all-too often taken up with battling the unreliable technology of that time – snail-paced upload speeds, never-ending download times and intermittent internet connections. While these innovators might have taken less than an hour to record their latest show, the drawn-out process of actually uploading content for the public to hear was sometimes enough to break the will of even the most determined amateur broadcaster, and it is easy to see the reason why. What was the point of going to all that trouble of putting it out there when your listeners couldn't even stream or download it? Even so, it seems bizarre that they were unable to foretell what a success story they would have on their hands. Only with the benefit of hindsight can we see that success was inevitable from the word go. The humble 'audioblog' has grown up and firmly taken root in popular culture.

B

The podcast's rise to fame only became possible after the mobile phone began its transformation from a clunky, unsophisticated brick with limited functionality to the virtual mini-computer smartphones of today. This progress has allowed the appeal of podcasts to steadily flourish. The two combine in perfect harmony; it is almost as if podcasts and smartphones were paired up and hand-crafted for on-the-go consumption, providing content that can be enjoyed equally as much when lying in the bath as when commuting, or even working through daily household chores. Herein lies the ultimate draw of podcasts: they are the perfect antidote to the fact that we modern consumers – and I use these words advisedly, counting myself among that number – can barely find time to brush our teeth, never mind sit down for a couple of hours and take in a film. As we move ever closer to 5G networks, and full podcasts have become instantaneously downloadable, these breathtaking advances in technology have, ironically, brought us back to a time when, rather than staring at screens, we listened to voices, independently lost in thought.

C

The great appeal for many is the fact that podcasters are usually people who are entirely unconnected with any sort of broadcasting or media company. In contrast, some commercial radio stations are now facing extinction after spending decades focussing more on profits than what their audience actually wants. An emphasis on advertising, the analysis of the latest data, clever predictions about which age or social group to target next, often with unashamedly financial intent, has left them out of touch with listeners. The fact is, podcasts have taken over precisely because they are all about allowing listeners to personalise and discover new content, rather than being told what they want to listen to. Instead of being preoccupied with ratings, they appeal to our individual interests, enthusiasms, confessions and a tradition that unites us all – great storytelling. Devoted listeners search the internet in the hope of uncovering the latest hidden gem, much in the same way as fans of vinyl used to flick through the shelves of record shops.

D

Sometimes it feels as if the podcasts you are currently working your way through have been recorded for you and you alone. Since the principal format is either of a conversation between two or three people chatting together, or of a main narrator talking directly to an audience of one, there is a familiarity created that speaks to our fundamental, innate desire for close interpersonal contact. Similarly, there is a tangible sense of pride and ownership when we share our latest 'must-listen' podcast with real-world friends. And when recommendations that really hit the spot come back to us from them, our friendship seems somehow to take an upward turn. And yet, as with all media phenomena, the inevitable fall will come; perhaps we have already, unknowingly, hit peak podcast. Indeed, some enthusiasts have announced that they are already turning away from the format, complaining bitterly about the increasing amount of advertising that has begun to corrupt this once-innocent medium.

In which section does the writer ...

1 give a reason why podcasts satisfy a basic human need?

2 point out a similarity in the behaviour of people in another situation?

3 admit the difficulty of correctly predicting whether something will do well or not?

4 mention some podcast listeners' annoyance at a current development?

5 describe how growth in the popularity of podcasts depended on developments in another technology?

6 admit to carrying out actions that he criticises?

7 question the motives of a particular group of people?

8 display understanding of the frustrations of others?

9 mention people's admiration of podcasters who remain independent?

10 suggest that the popularity of podcasting may already be coming to an end?

WRITING PART 2: EMAIL

You receive this email from an English-speaking friend.

I've just been offered work experience at a video games design company over the summer, which I'm really excited about. The problem is, they want me to come in for the whole of July – the month I'm supposed to be going on holiday with you. Should I say no? Will it upset you if we can't go away together?

Please let me know what you think.

---

1 Read the sentences. Which would be unlikely to gain credit from the examiner in answer to the question above?

A To whom it may concern,

B You needn't worry about upsetting me – I'm genuinely delighted for you.

C It would be a little annoying if you couldn't come, my mum and dad are really looking forward to hosting you for a few weeks.

D It's a good idea for you doing a video games design company job, I know will be good for you.

E Thinking about it, we'll be more in the mood to enjoy ourselves by that point, won't we?

F I can see why you're excited about the opportunity, however, you should get back to them when you finish reading this and say yes, though.

2 Match the assessment criteria and comments below to the sentences you selected in Exercise 1.

1 *Content*: not answering the question properly. Sentence ....

2 *Communicative Achievement*: inappropriate style for an email to a friend. Sentence ....

3 *Organisation*: unclear, difficult to understand. Sentence ....

4 *Language*: too basic for an Advanced candidate. Sentence ....

3 Read the answer to the exam question. Replace the underlined words and phrases with the informal phrasal verbs and idioms in the box.

get into	get together	jet off	kick off
pick up	put our heads together		tied down
turn down	wrapped up		

Hey … ,

First of all, huge congratulations on getting the placement. Wow! For as long as I've known you, you've wanted to ¹work within that industry. And when you bear in mind the fact that your next big plan is to study video game design at uni, this seems like the perfect way to ²initiate your career doing just that – think of all the new skills you'll be able to ³acquire! For goodness' sake, whatever you do, don't ⁴reject the opportunity just because you and I have a holiday planned.

You needn't worry about upsetting me – I'm genuinely delighted for you. Of course I'll be a bit sad that we can't spend time abroad together in July, but we can always ⁵reconsider this to choose some new dates. We're both free for pretty much the whole summer, so there's no real reason for us to be ⁶committed to going then.

I guess your work experience is a full-time thing, and we'd only be able to ⁷meet in the evenings after you've finished each day, which would mean that we won't see a lot of each other… So how about if we ⁸travel somewhere at the start of August? It could be a big celebration after you've ⁹completed your time at the design company. Thinking about it, we'll be more in the mood to enjoy ourselves by that point, won't we?

Again, well done, you! Let me know how you feel about August instead.

Speak soon,

Jaime

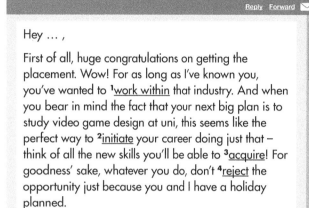

6 STRUCTURES AND LANDMARKS

GRAMMAR

1 Complete the sentences with the correct forms of the verb pairs in brackets. The first one has been done for you.

1 Most things worked okay when we moved in, but the cooker ___needed to be fixed___ (need/fix).

2 Before the first brick was laid, there were so many forms that _____ (have to/fill in).

3 The construction company were astonished at the sheer scale of the job they _____ (expect/achieve).

4 Only after they had received the engineers' report did they believe the designs _____ (would/approve).

5 We probably couldn't have sold our house without first _____ (get/make over).

2 Choose the correct options to complete the text.

When I was a teenager, I **(1)** *used to/would* dream of becoming an architect. Back then, I **(2)** *would/can* spend hours sitting in my room, sketching buildings I wanted to build someday. At school, even though I studied art, I was not **(3)** *supposed to/allowed to* do any projects on architecture. I think it's because my art teacher **(4)** *couldn't have/shouldn't have* helped me with them – she was a painter, really, and not very confident about technical drawing. It was a shame my parents couldn't afford to send me to the private school in our town – I definitely **(5)** *should have been/would have been* supported there. Anyway, whenever I **(6)** *was permitted to/was able to*, I **(7)** *had to/used to* take photos on my walk home, then sketch any architectural features I **(8)** *might have/must have* captured with my camera. Now, I realise that those days gave me the freedom to use my imagination. If I had gone to that other school, I **(9)** *could not have/might not have* developed my personal style in the same way and **(10)** *wouldn't have/mustn't have* become the famous architect I am today!

3 For each question, complete the second sentence so that it has a similar meaning to the first sentence, using the word given. Do not change the word given. Use between three and six words.

1 I don't agree with their decision to build that ugly multi-storey car park.
NEVER
That ugly multi-storey car park _____ built.

2 Apparently, the winner of the Interior Design Scholarship comes from Milan.
UNDERSTOOD
The winner of the Interior Design Scholarship _____ from Milan.

3 The lawyer claims that her client vandalised the monument as a form of protest.
ALLEGED
The suspect _____ vandalised the monument as a form of protest.

4 We made a mistake in not getting a signed contract before employing that builder.
OUGHT
We really _____ a signed contract before employing that builder.

5 Sam didn't remember to invite James to the event.
SUPPOSED
James _____ to the event, but Sam forgot.

VOCABULARY

1 Complete the sentences with the correct word from the box.

makeover	loft/attic	bungalows	demolish
DIY	hallway	tools	semi-detached house

1 My grandparents are moving house, but they only want to view .... because they can't climb stairs nowadays.

2 The council is planning to .... three historic buildings to make way for new flats.

3 Our interior designer did a great .... of our bedroom.

4 Right now we only use the .... for storage but we are thinking of converting it into another bedroom.

5 The most important thing for builders to remember is that they need to use the right .... for each job.

6 My mum loves doing .... She built some great bookcases over the weekend.

7 The one thing I love about living in a .... is that you can only ever be connected to noisy neighbours on one side.

8 Oh yes, our bathroom's down the .... to the left.

2 🔊 10 Listen to the speakers discussing building projects. Write the type of building/room which they are talking about.

1 ....
2 ....
3 ....
4 ....
5 ....

3 Join the sentence halves with the correct form of *get*, *have*, *make* or *do*.

1 In a drama school full of talent, my cousin stood out and…

2 Admittedly, owing to all the interruptions, it took a while for us…

3 Had I known you were thinking of becoming an engineer, I…

4 At the start of my course, I was sure that my architecture tutor…

5 While the 12th century church was a part of local history, it seems that the council…

6 If you ever travel to St Petersburg, you must…

7 You wouldn't have thought these small lights would create enough light for this attic, but they've certainly…

8 This city is exceptionally proud to be hosting the International Design Awards, which…

A … a point of visiting The Catherine Palace – the rococo design is astonishingly beautiful.

B … going on this project, but once the first brick was laid we felt more optimistic.

C … a name for herself as the most talented musical actress.

D … no option but to demolish it once it was deemed to be an unsafe structure.

E … something against me, but it turns out she was being strict to encourage me.

F … my utmost to help you find an internship at my company.

G … the job – it's a bright space now!

H … under way in August. They're a great attraction for residents and tourists alike.

PUSH YOURSELF C2

Find twelve words related to buildings in the word puzzle. Combine the words to make six phrases or collocations.

trajisobridgestuenttearthquakedipuhaxdrawingyuoamsleientofirevhnenerkjkjboardhuiquboom
ahiuncoopeyeootupsuspensionsplacatchingfyoukriguiotjhhazardionproofituepbuildinguiopwun

1 _____suspension bridge_____   4 _____

2 _____   5 _____

3 _____   6 _____

LISTENING PART 2

🔊 11 You will hear a student called Jess Erminite talking about a visit to Brasilia as part of her university course in architecture. For questions 1–8, complete the sentences with a word or short phrase.

Jess reveals that it was her focus on modern design **(1)** _____ that led her to success in the competition.

Jess decided to enter the competition when she learnt that only submissions from **(2)** _____ would be considered.

Since Brasilia is laid out into **(3)** _____ neighbourhoods, Jess explains, it is different from other major cities designed today.

Jess suggests that a sense of **(4)** _____ has been generated by the local people.

Jess expresses her admiration for the complete view of the **(5)** _____ that can be seen from the TV Tower.

Jess questions her guide's understanding of the **(6)** _____ of architecture.

Jess uses the word **(7)** _____ to describe her impression of the buildings at night.

Jess was surprised at the extent to which reflection has been made a **(8)** _____ feature.

1 Read the statements about the Speaking Part 2 exam. Which one is true?

1 Each candidate should speak for two minutes.
2 You should ask your partner clarification questions while they are speaking.
3 It is more important to describe the pictures than to speculate about them.
4 The examiner will ask you two questions after your partner's turn.
5 You should only describe two of the pictures.
6 If you haven't spoken for the full minute, inform the examiners by saying you are finished.

2 For which of the pictures (1–3) would the following vocabulary most likely be useful?

1 colour charts ....
2 hard hats ....
3 blueprints ....
4 residential property ....
5 step ladder ....
6 redecorate ....
7 deposit ....
8 mortgage ....
9 civil engineers ....
10 first-time buyers ....

3 🔊 12 Listen to Celine delivering a Part 2 turn for two of the pictures in Exercise 2. Tick the words and phrases in Exercise 2 that she uses.

4 🔊 12 Listen again and complete the gaps from the recording with the words you hear.

1 The first picture shows two people, ... a couple…
2 With the step ladder in shot, ... that they're giving the room a makeover.
3 .... that they are in their new house.
4 From the way they are sitting, ... that this could be their first house together…
5 … in this case, ... some blueprints of a building…
6 While this picture also shows a man and a woman, ... that they're colleagues…
7 … this is clearly not a residential property… .... they're civil engineers.

5 Using past modals verb forms to speculate can help you achieve a higher score in Speaking Part 2. Rewrite the extracts from the recording with the words in brackets.

1 Perhaps they've just arrived on site.
.... on site. (may/just/arrive)
2 Maybe they only moved into the place a short while before.
.... into the place a short while before. (might/only/move)
3 Maybe they got bored with their living room and decided to redecorate.
.... and decided to redecorate. (might/bored/their living room)
4 They have probably been getting excited about it all for some time.
.... about it all for some time. (may well/get excited)

7 BROADENING HORIZONS

GRAMMAR

1 Read the text and correct 14 mistakes with the use of articles.

While universities were not founded in West until Middle Ages, they did in fact exist in some parts of Asia in ancient times. More specifically, if you were alive in Taxila – located in northwest of India – around year 700 BC, you may well have been present for creation of the world's first university. Students were taught the number of subjects that still form a part of the modern-day education, such as philosophy, music and science (university was particularly renowned for a latter), and they began their education at age of 16. By a modern standards, the teaching apparatus was basic, to say least, but it would have been the very cosmopolitan environment in which to study, as the people came from all over Asia, the Middle East and Greece to study there.

2 Put the nouns from the word cloud below into the correct columns in the table.

importance
course
lecture
lesson
travel
degree
data
assignment
deadline
study
advice
fame
youth
science
project
evidence
imagination
quality
progress
graduate
research

3 Complete the sentences below with the correct form of nouns from the *Both* column. Then decide whether the noun is countable (C) or uncountable (U) in each sentence.

1 My English tutor has many admirable _____ , but patience isn't one of them.

C/U

2 The older you get, the more difficult it becomes to identify with the person you were in your _____ .

C/U

3 To a certain _____ , today's qualifications do not sufficiently prepare people for their future career.

C/U

4 Before the panic of his final year at university, Brian had rarely given much thought to his _____ .

C/U

5 Children learn best through play, using their vivid _____ to interpret and understand the world.

C/U

6 I learnt so much about the world when I was off on my _____ around South America.

C/U

COUNTABLE	UNCOUNTABLE	BOTH

VOCABULARY

1 Complete the sentences with the correct form of the word in brackets.

1 There has been much written about the _____ of study, with broad agreement about the importance of taking regular breaks. (psychologist)

2 Scientists have carried out a _____ survey of this newly-discovered site. (geologist)

3 Our company can introduce you to six _____ proven ways to improve memory. (scientist)

4 I find it enormously _____ to relax in a hot bath after a long day studying. (therapist)

5 In life, you absolutely must _____ on the opportunities that are put in front of you. (capitalism)

6 We were all out on the streets, protesting against the negative _____ policies of the current government. (environmentalism)

2 Complete the sentences with the adverbs in the box.

badly	deeply	heavily	strictly	utterly
vitally	widely			

1 Every student's learning is _____ influenced by the manner in which they are taught.

2 Einstein is _____ acknowledged to have had a huge influence in the field of physics.

3 There is a _____ limited number of tickets available for this afternoon's lecture.

4 The principal is _____ appalled by the behaviour of some protesters.

5 The lecturer's attempt at a joke was _____ received, and he was booed off the stage.

6 It cannot be stressed enough how _____ important it is to keep your study notes organised.

7 Some novels, which were once considered great works of art, are now _____ offensive to modern readers.

PUSH YOURSELF C2

Put the words in the correct order to form expressions with *bring* and *take*.

1 My boss has a poor attitude, but he certainly **a / table / brings / the / to / lot**.

2 There's no doubt that the encouragement Olivia received from her teacher this year **in / the / brought / has / best / out / her**.

3 If both parties agree to settle their dispute, we'll be looking to **close / a / matter / to / the / bring**.

4 When my tutor told me that my handwriting was like a six-year-old's, **but / way / couldn't / the / help / take / I / wrong / it**.

5 **A:** Peter has been put on a disciplinary by the principal.
   B: Good. **peg / two / should / a / him / That / take / down / or**.

6 After becoming the head of the Science department, **aback / was / taken / very / he** by the low morale of the teaching staff.

READING AND USE OF ENGLISH PART 4

For questions 1–6, complete the second sentence so that it has a similar meaning to the first sentence, using the word given. <u>Do not change the word given.</u> You must use between three and six words, including the word given.

1 It is entirely necessary that overseas students who want to study in the UK obtain a high-level English qualification.
OPTION
Overseas students who want to study in the UK _____ obtain a high-level English qualification.

2 Neil found it reassuring that people were enthusiastic about engaging with important social issues.
BY
Neil was _____ engaging with important social issues.

3 Simon, shouldn't you have sent off this job application yesterday?
SUPPOSED
Simon, wasn't this job application _____ sent off yesterday?

4 I was entirely happy with the quality of training I received on my course last week.
UNHAPPY
In _____ with the quality of training I received on my course last week.

5 Ivanka has always ignored people saying she couldn't be successful.
NOTICE
Ivanka _____ people saying she couldn't be successful.

6 When she was at school, Alice worked far harder than she does now.
NEARLY
Alice _____ as she did when she was at school.

SPEAKING PART 1

1 Use the sentences (A–I) to answer the two exam questions in the most logical way. There are three sentences that you do not need.

A It's given me a few ideas about what path I might eventually like to follow, but nothing concrete for now.

B I wouldn't say that there is anything specific for now, but I'm still at college so have plenty of time.

C Having said that, I recognise that I should probably learn to find other ways to cope with distraction.

D In a more general sense, I have started to look into options for doing something enjoyable and stimulating.

E That's why I find things more difficult in the classroom, as I can't do it without annoying other people.

F Nonetheless, obligation aside, there are definitely times when I can really lose myself in what I'm studying.

G I have little choice really, since I'm still at college and need to get my first qualifications.

H I'm not sure I'd necessarily describe it as 'enjoyment'. It's more of an obligation at the moment.

I I can't say that I'm the most focused student in the world, so I find listening to music really helps.

Question 1: Do you enjoy studying?
1 _H_   **2** _____   **3** _____

Question 2: What makes studying easier for you?
1 _____   **2** _____   **3** _____

2 🎧 13 Listen and check your answers to Exercise 1.

3 Use the remaining sentences from Exercise 1 to answer the exam question below.

Question 3: Is there anything that you are planning to study in the future?
1 _____   **2** _____   **3** _____

4 🎧 14 Listen and check your answer to Exercise 3.

WRITING PART 2: PROPOSAL

Your college has announced that it is making changes to the library in order to ensure that it is better suited to the needs of modern students. The principal is inviting students to send in a proposal outlining what changes should be made, and why, and how these changes will improve the study habits of those attending the college.

Write your proposal.

1 Complete the proposal headings (A–C) with the words in the box.

> available   existing   layout   materials
> review   space   technology   updating

```
●●● ◀▶                                    🔍 🏠
                              Reply  Forward  ✉
```

This proposal is intended to put forward recommendations for developing the college library in a way that would most benefit current and future students.

A _____ of _____ _____

In today's world, it is fair to say that the majority of students complete their homework on devices, and conduct their research online. Having said that, ¹dispose of all of these books? Not necessarily a good idea, and so I would suggest retaining around a quarter of existing stock. The books to be discarded should not simply be ²selected in a random way – by accessing library records, it would be possible to establish which are the ³ones which are borrowed most frequently, and should therefore be retained.

Additionally, while many of these learning materials themselves are somewhat outdated, students still often prefer the traditional method of note-taking with a pen and paper. ⁴You haven't supplied these for some time now. ⁵Restoring them to the library means happier students.

B _____ / _____ _____

At present, with the extensive use of shelves and cupboards in which books are kept, the number of students who can actually make use of the library at any one time is limited. Having conducted the audit as mentioned in the above section, you will not require many of these storage units, and you can dismantle and remove them. This will enable you to create a good deal of floor space. I would further recommend reducing the size of the librarians' desk.

C _____ _____

The PCs available are outdated and slow and ⁶you should replace them, certainly. The Wi-Fi is also unreliable in the library, so new routers and hubs are needed. ⁷This will ensure that people can study more effectively. It will also mean an increased likelihood of attracting a greater number of our students, ⁸some of those students have never been inside the library.

2 Read the teacher's notes below and improve the underlined sentences using the grammatical structures in bold, keeping as close to the original phrases as possible.

> Overall, this is a very good proposal, but it could be improved further for a higher score. The sections underlined and indicated with numbers in particular have the potential for more complex language.

1   THIRD CONDITIONAL (PASSIVE)
If all the books were disposed of, this/it would not necessarily be a good idea.

2   ADVERB + ADJECTIVE COLLOCATION

3   ADVERB + ADJECTIVE COLLOCATION

4   PASSIVE VERB FORM

5   SECOND CONDITIONAL (PASSIVE)

6   PASSIVE VERB FORM

7   INVERSION WITH *NOT ONLY...*

8   RELATIVE CLAUSE WITH *OF*

8 ON DEMAND

GRAMMAR

1 Read the conversation and then complete sentences 1–9 with the correct forms of the reporting verbs in the box and the underlined verbs.

Andrea: "Did you <u>manage</u> to catch that new series on *Flip TV*?"

Bogdan: "Do you <u>mean</u> *Blade of Sovereigns*, or the new police drama?"

Andrea: "Yeah, I'<u>m talking</u> about *Crime Scene 101*. Don't bother with *Blade of Sovereigns*, it starts well but soon turns into a boring, clichéd show."

Bogdan: "Wow, really? I have to say, I really <u>liked</u> the first episode. But I appreciate the advice."

Andrea: "Well, whatever you do, you absolutely must <u>start watching</u> *Crime Scene 101*."

Bogdan: "Right, I <u>will.</u> Definitely."

Andrea: "Believe me, you'll <u>find</u> very little to criticise in the whole show – in fact, there <u>was</u> only one negative for me."

Bogdan: "Oh, really? What'<u>s</u> that?"

Andrea: "I wish I <u>hadn't watched</u> the entire series in one day!"

add	advise	ask	assure	confirm	promise
query	regret	reveal	thank	urge	wonder

1 Andrea _____ if Bogdan _____ to catch a new series on *Flip TV*.

2 Bogdan _____ whether Andrea _____ *Blade of Sovereigns* or the new police drama.

3 Andrea _____ that _____ about *Crime Scene 101*, and _____ Bogdan against watching *Blade of Sovereigns*.

4 Bogdan _____ that he _____ the first episode, but _____ Andrea for her advice.

5 Andrea _____ Bogdan _____ *Crime Scene 101*.

6 Bogdan _____ that _____ watch it.

7 Andrea _____ Bogdan that _____ very little to criticise in the whole show, and _____ that there _____ only one negative for her.

8 Bogdan _____ what that _____ .

9 Andrea _____ the entire series in one day.

2 Read the sentences below and correct the mistakes where necessary. Tick (✔) any sentences which are correct.

1 If you would have been kind enough to show me to my seat, I would have been able to get comfortable before the film started.

2 I do believe that, if given the freedom to operate unrestricted, the press in this country will get worse.

3 Paco was just trying to be funny when he posted that meme, but after the awful reaction he got, I bet he wishes he didn't now.

4 Can you remind Simona that I'm still waiting for her media studies homework, whether you happen to see her?

5 I know watching six consecutive hours of a series is bad for me, but once I've started, that's it. I just wish turning the TV off was something I could do.

6 If the footage had been approved by the editor on the news desk, the public might be aware of what happened.

7 What would your choice have been, if you were asked what your favourite streaming service is now?

8 You know, I'd love to be an influencer with millions of followers. If only I knew where to start!

VOCABULARY

1 Complete the words in the dialogue with the correct letters. The first letters are given to help you.

A: Did you see the documentary on the positive influence of social media in politics last night?

B: Yes, a very interesting **(1)** a＿＿＿＿＿＿＿＿ ＿＿＿＿＿ of the situation. I thought the **(2)** p＿＿＿＿ ＿＿＿＿＿ ＿＿＿ ＿＿＿ ＿＿＿ ＿＿＿ went into the issue in great depth, and allowed the guests plenty of time to air their views.

A: I completely agree. I particularly liked the technology **(3)** c＿＿＿ ＿＿ ＿＿ ＿＿ ＿＿ ＿＿＿ ＿＿ ＿＿ ＿＿ ＿＿; he had a great way of making complex situations seem simple.

B: This is the sort of thing that isn't given enough **(4)** c＿＿＿ ＿＿ ＿＿ ＿＿ ＿＿ in the mainstream media, there's so much negativity about how easily influenced people are by a few paid-for ads.

2 Complete the sentences with the correct form of the words in the box.

casting	commentary	contestant
highlights	script	subtitle

1 You don't have to tell me everything about what happened, just give me the edited ＿＿＿＿＿ .

2 Actors often have to attend dozens of ＿＿＿＿＿ sessions before they are offered a substantial part.

3 The ＿＿＿＿＿ on the match last night was awful. It was clearly biased towards the current champions.

4 It's often difficult for me to enjoy films with ＿＿＿＿＿ . My brain just ends up reading and not watching what's happening on the screen.

5 I've read the ＿＿＿＿＿ for the new comedy series and it's absolutely hilarious.

6 I'd love to have a go at being a game show ＿＿＿＿＿ and try to win a lot of money.

3 Choose the correct options to complete the sentences.

1 In an astonishing turnaround, all of the major newspapers have suddenly *refused/denied* to support the president.

2 After extensive rumours, Therese d'Anjou has released a statement to *clarify/claim* that she will be stepping down as Channel 12's Foreign Correspondent next year.

3 There are so many adverts invading my profile page these days, all *releasing/promoting* some product that I briefly searched for ages ago.

4 We take your feedback seriously, and are inviting members to *put forward/negotiate* any suggestions that could improve your user experience on our platform.

5 The social media platform *Mii-Chat* has sought to *reassure/appeal* users that, despite the latest security breach, their personal data is entirely safe.

6 When the latest scandal surfaced, the politician claimed that he had been *misled/warned* by his advisors, and offered to resign.

PUSH YOURSELF C2

Complete the sentences with the correct form of the reporting verbs in the box.

allege	butt in	cheer on	deem	go on	own up

1 Alain Guerra was a fantastic player, but as a commentator he's awful – he can't stop himself from ＿＿＿＿＿ when other people are discussing a match.

2 The two teams will ＿＿＿＿＿ by somewhere in the region of two million armchair fans in Saturday's final.

3 I only watched that new comedy series after Nikki kept ＿＿＿＿＿ about how funny it was. I wish I hadn't wasted my time.

4 The woman who was arrested ＿＿＿＿＿ to have sold trade secrets to hostile foreign governments.

5 Given that nobody ＿＿＿＿＿ to breaking the common room TV, the college finally decided to replace it.

6 The novel *Animal Farm* was banned in many countries after ＿＿＿＿＿ to be inappropriate for public consumption.

 ⊘ 15 **You will hear three different extracts. For questions 1–6, choose the answer (A, B or C) which fits best according to what you hear. There are two questions for each extract.**

Extract One

1 When discussing an online article they have both read, the friends agree that
    A teenagers have a mature attitude towards social media.
    B the writer is being unfair in their criticism of influencers.
    C influencers use social media in a widely inclusive way.

2 In the woman's opinion, the problem with using influencers to advertise on social media is
    A the lack of sincerity shown to consumers.
    B the excessive fees charged by the influencers.
    C the obsessive behaviour of the people following influencers.

Extract Two

3 Which research findings into fake news does the man question?
    A that people lack awareness of the tricks used by news publishers
    B that people often trust stories that correspond to their opinions
    C that people find it an entertaining distraction from reality

4 How does the woman respond to her friend's complaint?
    A She recommends reading a wider variety of sources for news.
    B She suggests trying out a technical solution.
    C She can't understand his decision to turn away from current affairs.

Extract Three

5 What point does the woman make about the project she is doing?
    A How grateful she is for some advice she received from a friend
    B How appreciative she is of contemporary resources for learning
    C How repetitive she found doing all the research

6 The man says that since starting to watch online talks he has become
    A more creative in his general approach to study skills.
    B less embarrassed about his lack of technical proficiency.
    C more willing to collaborate with his peers on his course.

1 Read the review and choose the best title (A–C).

A Where would I be without *Flip TV*?
B The benefits of a *Flip TV* subscription
C Streaming services are taking over the world

← →

Twenty years ago, *Flip TV* first made a name for itself as a reliable DVD delivery service. How times change. Today, in a crowded field of online streaming providers, ¹it stands head and shoulders above its competitors, and it is not difficult to see why.

A major plus point of *Flip TV* is that it has an intriguing and ²ever-expanding list of titles, both old and new, and there is very much something for everyone. Are you an ³aficionado of French cinema? You won't be disappointed. Enthusiastic viewer of nature documentaries? There are enough of those to keep you staring at elephants and volcanoes for ⁴days on end. Pretty much every genre is covered, and the programmes within each category are rotated on a regular basis, keeping the viewing lists fresh. What's more, *Flip TV* has this year started ⁵putting out its own shows, many of which I believe can ⁶hold their own against anything produced by major studios.

Another of its main attractions is its genuinely intelligent recommendation system, which I believe solves a common complaint: most streaming services have a way of pushing titles into your feed that, frankly, do your head in and someone would have to pay you to watch. *Flip TV* is different – it's almost as if it knows you inside out. This is helped along by an initial, detailed questionnaire you have to fill in. It takes some time to complete, but I'd thoroughly recommend doing so. You will reap the rewards of this in the end.

So, what more could you possibly need? Never before have I happened upon a TV service that is delivered in such an intuitive way, with such a vast array of entertainment options.

2 Match the idiomatic phrases in the first two paragraphs of the review (1–6) to the meanings below (A–F).

A a very long time ....
B compete with ....
C it is much better than ....
D constantly growing ....
E producing ....
F fan ....

3 Read the final two paragraphs and find idiomatic paraphrases of the words and phrases below.

1 be incredibly annoying ....
2 you have no interest in watching ....
3 is very familiar with what you like ....
4 enjoy the benefits ....
5 discovered ....
6 very wide range ....

9 CULTURAL CONTRIBUTION

GRAMMAR

1 Put the words in bold in the correct order to complete the sentences.

1 Surprisingly, many ancient societies were **open / at / least / as / alternative lifestyles / as / to** their modern equivalents.
_____

2 Taylor Swift is **most / the / easily / recognisable / of / one / pop stars** today.
_____

3 I couldn't believe how many courses there are at Italian weddings. It was **fullest / been / I / ever / by / far / the / have** after a meal. _____

4 Our school trip to the British Museum, **as / my / was / it / as / fascinating / classmates / for**, bored me to tears.

5 The **more / my / about / discover / I /** family history, **become / keener / I / the** to pay a genealogist to research it properly for me. _____

6 While the festival was great fun, **not / to / times / the / it / of / go / best / was**, I'm afraid. It rained almost constantly.
_____

7 The people I met on my travels were **a / friendlier / great / than / deal** I had been led to believe.
_____

2 Choose the correct options to complete the sentences below.

1 There is less pressure these days on people to get married and *since/thus*, more people than ever are deciding not to do so.

2 *So that/So as to* ensure that she didn't miss any of the Queen's parade, Sandra spent the night at the start of the procession route.

3 Many local residents move out of their homes during the weeks of carnival *because of/because* the incessant noise.

4 *As a consequence of/As a result* there being a waiting list of three months for tickets, I don't expect I'll get to see that new Frida Kahlo exhibition.

5 *Since/So* holding the temporary Picasso retrospective, the museum has welcomed more visitors than in the previous five years.

6 There will be an extra bank holiday this year, *because/so that* the king's 50th birthday can be commemorated.

7 The road closure in the centre of town, which will run from 14.00 today, is *due to/because* the Divali parade that is to begin at 17.30.

8 Your sociology project needs to be handed in next week, so it might *as consequence/therefore* be a good idea to start researching it now.

VOCABULARY

1 Complete the sentences with a prepositional phrase. Use the word in brackets to help you.

1 I'm completely _____ _____ _____ to explain why anyone still visits museums – they're so dull. (*loss*)

2 It was nothing _____ _____ that 200 people were at my wedding – we have a huge family. (*ordinary*)

3 Although the library is quite informal, _____ _____ _____ is it permitted for anyone to bring in food or drink. (*means*)

4 We're launching a new campaign to raise money _____ _____ _____ the Genie Foundation. (*aid*)

5 Paolo was ill on my wedding day, but thankfully, George stepped in _____ _____ _____ and gave a great best man's speech. (*notice*)

6 I was _____ _____ _____ that the Haka was part of Aboriginal culture, but I was wrong. (*impression*)

7 The intricate detail on the dresses in this display are entirely _____ _____ _____ the style of that time. (*keeping*)

8 In previous centuries, it would have been _____ _____ for a monarch to talk to their subjects face-to-face. (*question*)

2 Use the word given in capitals at the end of some of the lines to form a word that fits in the gap in the same line.

It is difficult to imagine visiting Greece without a trip to one sort of temple or another. From the **(1)** _____ Mycenae, in whose city walls the Cyclops is said to have roamed, and where you can go for a browse in one of the most interesting **(2)** _____ museums anywhere in the world, to the world renowned Acropolis of Athens, which is **(3)** _____ in its sheer scale. Even the most avid traveller would find it impossible to explore each and every shrine to Greek **(4)** _____ .	**LEGEND** **ARCHAEOLOGY** **MONUMENT** **MYTH**
While these attractions buzz with life and laughter today, some of them were not always thus, being places where the **(5)** _____ of animals was commonplace. Goats, most frequently, were the typical subjects to be **(6)** _____ offered up to the Gods.	**SACRED** **RITUAL**
Of course, with the **(7)** _____ of society, this type of practice was gradually abandoned, but the plentiful food that came after an animals' unfortunate end is still celebrated and enjoyed today during **(8)** _____ feasts.	**SECULAR** **COMMEMORATE**

PUSH YOURSELF C2

Match the parts of the comparative structures, then use them to complete the sentences below.

any sweeter	deep-rooted that
as if	opening weekend as
no more	a sound than
not be any—	valid than
so	— more different
such a successful	to suggest

1 People often think that because my sister and I both study Art and Photography, we must be really similar, but we could _____ if we tried.

2 Many cultural norms are _____ people rarely stop to question whether they are still relevant to modern society.

3 Classical music is _____ K-Pop in terms of its status as an international art form.

4 In Da Vinci's world-renowned painting, the *Mona Lisa* is smiling _____ that she already knows how famous she will become one day.

5 Never before has cinema seen _____ for *Avengers: Endgame*, which took over $1.2 billion worldwide.

6 There cannot be _____ a Bechstein grand piano, played by someone who really knows what they are doing.

1 For questions 1–8 below, read the text and think of the word that best fits the gap. Use only one word in each gap. There is an example at the beginning (0).

Write your answers IN CAPITAL LETTERS on the separate answer sheet.

ANSWER:	(0)		A	S														

Elephants have thousands of years of experience **(0)** _____ cultural icons, proud and dominant features in symbolism and mythology throughout history. Images of early elephants were painted onto the walls of caves inhabited **(1)** _____ our ancestors, suggesting that these magnificent beasts were not simply hunted for food, but also held **(2)** _____ the highest regard – idolised, even. In modern times, certain festivals require them to be dressed in glorious, colourful decoration, often to symbolise royalty. In fact, so dominant is their presence that it is impossible to conceive **(3)** _____ some local cultures existing without them. And **(4)** _____ become such an omnipresent feature of life and culture over the centuries, this looks unlikely to change **(5)** _____ time soon.

Perhaps this all comes **(6)** _____ the fact that their appeal is both aesthetic and functional. Even today, elephants are still used for heavy labour in India in **(7)** _____ of machinery. They also appear in modern metaphors, **(8)** _____ being a symbol of unspoken problems in the phrase 'the elephant in the room'.

LISTENING PART 4

🔊 16 **You will hear five short extracts in which people talk about unusual family traditions.**

TASK ONE

For questions 1–5, choose from the list (A–H) the reason each speaker gives for the tradition becoming established.

A to renew old acquaintances
B to resolve ongoing arguments
C to keep inter-personal relations polite
D to deal with an awkward situation
E to revive an abandoned project
F to diminish the effects of a traumatic event
G to address an emotional need
H to provide amusement for others

Speaker 1	**1** _____
Speaker 2	**2** _____
Speaker 3	**3** _____
Speaker 4	**4** _____
Speaker 5	**5** _____

TASK TWO

For questions 6–10, choose from the list (A–H) how each speaker now feels about the tradition.

A upset by the memories it stirs
B ashamed of how silly it is
C dismissive of its intended purpose
D admiring of the time it took to be established
E doubtful of its ongoing necessity
F eager for the opportunity to re-enact it
G proud of how unusual it is
H grateful for its continued presence

Speaker 1	**6** _____
Speaker 2	**7** _____
Speaker 3	**8** _____
Speaker 4	**9** _____
Speaker 5	**10** _____

WRITING PART 2: REPORT

Your English class has recently gone on a museum tour in the town or city where you live. The principal of the school has asked you for a report.

Your report should briefly describe the tour, comment on how effective it was in engaging students throughout their visit, and suggest ways in which it could be improved.

Write your report.

1 Choose the best heading for each section (A–D).

1 Museums: Should we return?
2 Introduction
3 Focusing on the future: _our_ future
4 What this report is about
5 Evaluation of the tour
6 Who we met and what we saw
7 Itinerary
8 Recommendations
9 Route/Timings
10 What we did on our trip

2 Read the phrases (1–8) taken from the report. Is sentence A or B more likely to gain credit from the examiner? Think about grammar and register when choosing your answers.

1 **A** focusing on what people most liked about it
  B focusing on content and the way in which it was received
2 **A** engaged the students immediately with
  B immediately got everyone on his side by telling us
3 **A** we were moved onto
  B the guide took us all to
4 **A** we had put together
  B had been compiled
5 **A** an overly long time
  B ages and ages
6 **A** Although it wasn't quite as successful as the others
  B While it was not quite as much of a resounding success
7 **A** has much to offer in terms of a return visit
  B would totally be worth a return visit
8 **A** depressing topics
  B bleak themes

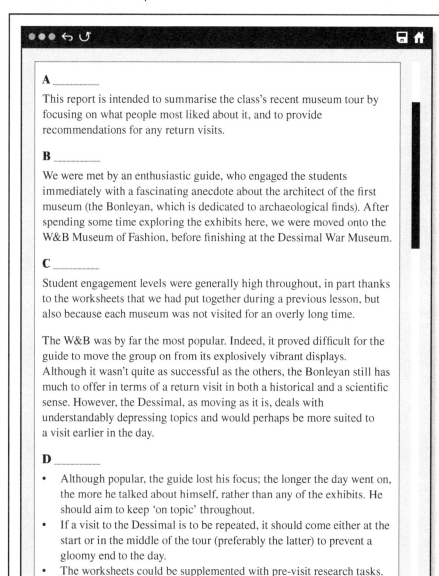

A ....

This report is intended to summarise the class's recent museum tour by focusing on what people most liked about it, and to provide recommendations for any return visits.

B ....

We were met by an enthusiastic guide, who engaged the students immediately with a fascinating anecdote about the architect of the first museum (the Bonleyan, which is dedicated to archaeological finds). After spending some time exploring the exhibits here, we were moved onto the W&B Museum of Fashion, before finishing at the Dessimal War Museum.

C ....

Student engagement levels were generally high throughout, in part thanks to the worksheets that we had put together during a previous lesson, but also because each museum was not visited for an overly long time.

The W&B was by far the most popular. Indeed, it proved difficult for the guide to move the group on from its explosively vibrant displays. Although it wasn't quite as successful as the others, the Bonleyan still has much to offer in terms of a return visit in both a historical and a scientific sense. However, the Dessimal, as moving as it is, deals with understandably depressing topics and would perhaps be more suited to a visit earlier in the day.

D ....

- Although popular, the guide lost his focus; the longer the day went on, the more he talked about himself, rather than any of the exhibits. He should aim to keep 'on topic' throughout.
- If a visit to the Dessimal is to be repeated, it should come either at the start or in the middle of the tour (preferably the latter) to prevent a gloomy end to the day.
- The worksheets could be supplemented with pre-visit research tasks.

10 LIVING LIFE TO THE FULL

GRAMMAR

1 Read the sentences about Tyrone Bogues. Tick (✔) the one which is grammatically correct. Correct the underlined parts of the other five sentences.

1 <u>Although far smaller than his opponents</u>, Bogues still managed to have a successful career in the NBA.

2 While most of his opponents towered over him, <u>however Bogues still managed</u> to be a professional in the NBA.

3 Bogues had a relatively successful career in the NBA, <u>despite of his height</u>.

4 <u>However he may have been short</u>, Bogues still managed to make a name for himself in the NBA.

5 Bogues spent many successful years playing in the NBA, <u>whereas he was far shorter</u> than everyone else on the court.

6 Bogues was only 1.6m tall. <u>This did however not stop him</u> from enjoying a 14-year career in the NBA.

2 Look at the blog posts in response to the question. Use substitution or ellipsis for the underlined sections to avoid repetition. For some you simply need to cut words but others may also need to add words from the box.

one	so	such

1 ~~there is a huge degree of hand-to-eye coordination involved in playing darts~~ **such**

2 ....

3 ....

4 ....

5 ....

6 ....

Home   About   Blogs   Reviews

WHICH SPORT WOULD YOU INCLUDE IN THE OLYMPIC GAMES?

Despite many people viewing it as a game rather than a sport, there is a huge degree of hand-to-eye coordination involved in playing darts. As [1]<u>there is a huge degree of hand-to-eye coordination involved in playing darts</u>, it can be compared with archery, for instance, and must be considered.
Posted 1:15pm

Skateboarding comes with many recommendations as an activity that can be done anywhere and, to a certain extent, [2]<u>if you want to do it anywhere, you certainly can do it anywhere</u>. BMX racing has made it onto the list of Olympic Sports, so I can't see why skateboarding [3]<u>hasn't made it</u> as well.
Posted 11.50am

Chess, unbelievably, has never been played at the Olympic Games and I for one would be delighted if the authorities introduced it the next time around. [4]<u>Introducing it the next time around</u> would allow one of the world's most noble and ancient games to gain new audiences across the world.
Posted 9.10am

For me, it's cricket. There's this stereotype that each match takes days to complete, and, yes, [5]<u>some matches take days to complete</u>, but one-day cricket would be perfect for the Olympics. If you're looking for a sport with worldwide appeal to add to the list, that certainly is [6]<u>a sport with worldwide appeal</u>.
Posted 7.40pm

There are so many amazing, unacknowledged sports to choose from, but [7]<u>which amazing, unacknowledged sport</u> would I suggest? I find it astonishing that polo isn't included. The organisers already have events for other equestrian disciplines, so I find it bizarre that they [8]<u>don't have an event</u> with polo.
Posted 4.30pm

VOCABULARY

1 Choose the correct options to complete the sentences. Sometimes more than one answer is possible.

1 On Saturday, Atletico defeated their bitter *rivals/enemies/competitors*, Real Madrid, in a tense local derby.

2 As I watched Usain Bolt run the Men's 100 metres final in 2008, I knew immediately that I was *watching/spectating/witnessing* sporting history being created.

3 Across the world, there are now more *viewers/spectators/audience* watching online sports than there are who actually attend live matches.

4 In today's final, the Belfast Giants *dominated/outplayed/defeated* their opponents, the Sheffield Steelers, in a close 4–3 victory.

5 With one race left, Lewis Hamilton is the current *champion/victor/leader* in this year's Formula One championship – but only just.

6 In Wimbledon 2010, it took John Isner 11 hours and 5 minutes to finally *eliminate/win/defeat* Nicolas Mahut and progress to the second round.

PUSH YOURSELF C2

Complete the interview with a football coach with the phrases in the box.

below the belt	jump the gun	on the home stretch
the ball is in his/her/their court		touch base	under par

A: It's been a long season, but surely you must feel like you're **(1)** _____ now?

B: Well, I don't want to **(2)** _____ , but I think we're finally safe from relegation into the league below.

A: And what about your position as manager next season?

B: I'm going to **(3)** _____ with the owner on Monday to find out what he's planning for the club.

A: So, you'd like to stay on?

B: I would. **(4)** _____ as it's his club, but yes, I'd love to stay.

A: Even though the team's performance, under your management, has been very much **(5)** _____ for most of their games this year?

B: Well, the fact is that we've got enough points to stay in this difficult league, so I think that analysis of the team is a bit **(6)** _____ , actually.

2 Write the correct verb form of the nouns and adjectives in the box in the table according to their suffix.

~~breadth~~ bright clarity classification deaf depth diverse example false justification less like quantity weak worse unity

-IFY	*-EN*
	broaden

3 Complete the sentences with the correct form of the words from Exercise 2.

1 Play at the French Open has been temporarily abandoned because of the rain, but it looks as if the weather is due to _____ up before too long.

2 Our new football coach is trying really hard to _____ the team so they play well together.

3 It's difficult to _____ how much I love badminton. Given the chance, I'd play it every minute of every day.

4 As the players walked out of the tunnel, they felt as if they _____ by the noise the crowd was making.

5 There is no doubt about it, Roger Federer _____ dedication to his sport. The way he trains and keeps himself at peak fitness means he is a role model for all young players.

6 Star City have been deducted 10 points after an investigation found that they _____ several of their players' work permits.

7 I would like the referee to _____ why he gave the player a red card.

8 Ellen van Dijk's playing style _____ to that of her father and trainer, Benjamin, as they both hit the ball in the same way.

You are going to read extracts from four articles in which sports scientists give their views on achieving sporting excellence. For questions 1–4, choose from the extracts A–D. The sports scientists may be chosen more than once.

A

Now and then, while we are watching our favourite sporting idols produce a magical performance, there is a temptation to think to ourselves, 'that could be me'. This seems to be especially true for those of us who obsess about one sport above all others. The truth is that the pursuit of excellence enjoys such an idealistic hold over participants and fans alike that it seems unfair not to allow ourselves these odd moments of self-delusion. After all, popular wisdom maintains that regardless of work ethic or dedication, an athlete's innate ability will always be the decisive factor in sporting success, and it is certainly tempting to fall for this notion. However, the astonishing levels of commitment required to reach the top should not be under-estimated, nor should we lose sight of the vital role of being in the right place at the right time when attempting to define what it takes to hit the sporting heights.

B

It may well be time to put to bed the argument that joining the ranks of the sporting elite requires a laser-guided focus on an individual sport almost from infancy, since research suggests that the path to sporting excellence may actually develop from early training in a number of different sporting disciplines. As for the 10,000-hour rule, the idea that excellence in any field can be achieved with enough practice, it is astonishing that serious commentators continue to endorse such a theory, given that it has been side-lined by more solid research over the past decade. Indeed, there is now a compelling body of evidence that indicates genetic predisposition is essential to higher-level sporting ability. As such, it is entirely understandable that those watching from the paid seats may misguidedly convince themselves they possess that 'special something' within themselves to emulate their sporting heroes.

C

The increased performance levels of modern-day athletes compared to their predecessors have undoubtedly been made possible by improvements in sports science and training. Theories such as achieving expertise through spending 10,000 hours of practice on one discipline may seem cold and analytical and not at all in keeping with the magic and romance that inspires many to seek to imitate their idols. Nevertheless, as sports fans we have to stop deceiving ourselves. Talent on its own means nothing without dedication and sacrifice. To believe otherwise is naive. The vast majority of successful athletes settle on a sport at a young enough age to allow themselves time to amass the necessary quantity of practice and rarely, if ever, stray from their intitial choice. Hence, when it comes to them achieving sporting greatness, it is fair to say that most top sportspeople have made their own luck.

D

The idea that the sporting elite are a class apart owing to some untrainable, natural ability is one that is firmly rooted in the public imagination, and difficult to shift. While it is clearly true that such an ability is arguably an advantage, there are other factors which contribute. Certainly, an athlete needs a lot of things to go their way to give them the best possible chance of rising up the ranks, such as avoiding injuries, or enjoying a healthy dose of good fortune in particular. Even so, there is no guarantee of reaching such heights. The other missing piece of the puzzle which enables sportspeople to get to that point can be described by the theory of 'deliberate practice'. Ultimately, it is this long-term, purposeful and systematic repetition of the skills unique to a particular sport that brings the highest levels of success.

Which writer

1 provides a different idea from the others about the significance of natural talent in sporting success?

2 expresses a similar opinion to C about the advantage gained by concentrating on one sport?

3 holds a different view from D about the extent to which unpredictable events play a part in eventual success?

4 agrees with A's attitude towards spectators who liken themselves to professional sportspeople?

WRITING PART 1: ESSAY

Your class has watched a discussion on the role of sport in society. You have made the notes below:

> The role of sport in society:
> • uniting social groups
> • encouraging healthy lifestyles
> • educating younger people
>
> Some opinions expressed in the discussion:
>
> "Sport brings people together from all areas of society."
>
> "Sport helps keep a healthy mind and body."
>
> "Playing sport allows kids to learn about winning and losing."
>
> Write an essay for your tutor discussing two of the roles of sport in society in your notes. You should explain which role is more significant, giving reasons to support your opinion.
>
> You may, if you wish, make use of the opinions expressed in the discussion, but you should use your own words as far as possible.

1 Complete the introduction to the essay with the words in the box.

> encouraging   participating   positive   powerful   supporting

> There is a **(1)** .... argument that society could not function without sport. There are so many **(2)** .... sides to **(3)** .... in sport, two of which are **(4)** .... people in their quest to become more healthy and **(5)** .... people from different walks of life to come together.
>
> It is difficult to understate the importance of sport in maintaining high levels of fitness. So many people today have difficulty in performing everyday tasks that would otherwise cause them no problems, were they to be physically healthy. Further to this, someone in poor shape has less chance of an extended lifespan. Sport can often provide a motivation to ensure that they live life to the full. If any further proof were needed, the simple fact is that the greater the amount of time a person spends on physical activity, the more chance they have of feeling in good shape mentally.

2 Rearrange the sentences below to form a logical third paragraph to the essay.

> **(A)** This happens on an even greater scale during major international events. **(B)** Following on from this, I would also suggest that one of the main aims of sport is to allow people to bond with one another, regardless of their age, beliefs or status. **(C)** Rarely do you find any other aspect of life in which this is so. **(D)** At these times, entire countries come together, all because of sport. **(E)** For instance, if you were to visit a football stadium on a matchday, you would no doubt find two people who are complete opposites in so many ways, but who have become close purely because of their shared love for their team.

3 Choose the best sentence (A–C) to start the essay conclusion.

> .... , I would argue that its single most important function is that it provides a way in which people can stay fit and healthy, which is becoming increasingly difficult in the modern world.
>
> **A**: To sum up, while it is certainly true that sport is a valuable tool in teaching children about the value of winning and losing
>
> **B**: To sum up, while it is certainly true that sport plays a huge part in bringing unity to society
>
> **C**: To sum up, while it is certainly true that sport plays a big role in helping rich and poor people get on with each other

11 A STEADY JOB

1 Read the sentences and choose the correct type of emphasis (A–D).

A fronting	B cleft sentence	C auxiliary verb	D inversion

1 Anna is a nightmare to work with, but she does get results. ....
2 What I want to tell you is, your jobs are safe, despite a disappointing sales performance this month. ....
3 A very good meeting, that was. I feel like we really covered a lot of ground. ....
4 At no point during her interview did Frida realise that someone else had already been given the job. ....
5 It's not ideal, constantly travelling abroad for work, but I do love flying business class. ....
6 No sooner had Alan got promoted than he found out the company was under administration. ....
7 It was the company car that sealed the deal for Matteo, and he decided to take the job. ....
8 In front of him stood his boss. Joel knew from the look on her face that he was in trouble. ....

2 Read the sentences and correct the mistakes with emphasis. One of the sentences is correct.

1 When Hiro arrived at work that morning, little he realised that he was going to be made redundant.
2 Hardly has the meeting began when Simon realised he had left his notes on the train.
3 In no way young people are to blame for the lack of job opportunities these days.
4 Almost immediately they knew had hired the right person.
5 It was his confidence that convinced everyone he would one day be a successful entrepreneur.

3 Rewrite the sentences using the words at the beginning of the second sentences.

1 The takeover will be completed when the company accountants have approved it.
ONLY WHEN ....

2 In any interview he had ever had, Gareth always forgot to ask his own questions.
NOT ONCE ....

3 You wouldn't be here now if I hadn't taken a chance and given you the job.
HAD ....

4 Yves resigned and almost immediately started to feel less stressed.
NO SOONER ....

5 It's not common for people to stay in the same job for life these days.
RARELY ....

6 We will only stop advertising the job when we find the perfect candidate for the role.
NOT UNTIL ....

VOCABULARY

1 Complete the multi-word verbs in the text with options from the box in the correct form. You can use some of the options more than once.

| up | on | take | let | back | help | burn | down | work | through |

Home | About | Search

Maria left university a year ago, and has been in the same company ever since. Here are her three golden rules to ensure recent graduates keep their first job after landing it.

Cut **(1)** _____ on socialising for a while if you want to make a good impression. You'll find yourself **(2)** _____ out if you go to dinner with your friends every night and have to be in work early the next day. You certainly won't make a good impression if you keep turning **(3)** _____ late two or three times a week.

Your boss may well be extremely busy, so ask if there is anything you can **(4)** _____ them out with. It's definitely worth **(5)** _____ on extra tasks, even if you have to stay **(6)** _____ at the end of the day. You'll soon end **(7)** _____ in their good books. Don't promise too much, though, otherwise you won't have time to get **(8)** _____ everything, and you'll end up **(9)** _____ your boss down.

There will come a point when you'll feel exhausted and unappreciated, and you'll wish you were back at university. But you can't let that feeling **(10)** _____ over your life. Carry **(11)** _____ , keep working hard and you'll **(12)** _____ it out in the end.

2 Replace the words in bold in the sentences with a synonym. The first letters are given in brackets to help you.

1 It is astonishing to think that billionaire businessman Alan Fructose was once so broke that he couldn't afford to **recruit** a suit to wear to meetings. (h _____)

2 I gave my pitch to the new CEO. She didn't respond in an entirely positive way, but I had been expecting her to **sack** my idea before I'd finished. (d _____)

3 Becky will be on maternity **time-off** for the next 6 months, so you will be taking on some of her responsibilities. (l _____)

4 All members of **personnel** must attend a health and safety training course when they first start. (s _____)

5 Edie couldn't believe that her bitter rival, Susanna, had been **elevated** ahead of her and was now her boss. (p _____)

6 Generally speaking, a company decides in January or April who is going to get a pay **growth**, usually set at around 3%. (r _____)

7 As much as I'd love to have bought that house, the bank wouldn't give me a mortgage as my annual **wage** is too low. (s _____)

8 Jeanette's hard work at university paid off – she is now enjoying a very lucrative **vocation** in the financial services industry. (c _____)

PUSH YOURSELF C2

Complete the idioms in the sentences. The first letters are given to help you.

1 The new Prime Minister has claimed that she will be o _____ t _____ f _____ **line** in the battle against tax avoidance and plans to bring in harsher legislation.

2 Luisa knew she hadn't been working very hard lately, but it was a bit o _____ o _____ **line** for her business partner to suggest that she was only in it for the money.

3 Although I don't mention him by name, it's clear if you r _____ b _____ t _____ **lines** of my resignation letter that I blame my manager for my decision to leave the company.

4 As a family-run firm, we prioritise the wellbeing of our staff. But, **the b _____ line** is, we still need to make money, and that hasn't been happening for a while.

5 Company bosses have been urged not to t _____ such a t _____ **line o** _____ punctuality, as disciplining staff for being ten minutes late is often counter-productive.

6 I went to see the college careers advisor and she encouraged me to go into the finance industry. It's hard to f _____ **her line o** _____ r _____ on this because I'm awful at maths!

7 Our business has done better than expected this year, so we should celebrate. I was thinking something a _____ t _____ **lines o** _____ a company barbecue in the courtyard.

8 I was always getting asked to do chores for my old boss, but I d _____ t _____ **line at** doing her laundry. I'm not that desperate for a job!

LISTENING PART 3

17 You will hear an interview in which two ex-producers of a successful TV series, Eva Bradley and Eric Gates, talk about their experiences on the show and their new business consultancy. For questions 1–6, choose the answer (A, B, C or D) which best fits according to what you hear.

1 Eva explains that, at the time they started working on the show, she and Eric
  - **A** lacked confidence in their ability to succeed.
  - **B** relied on their experience of producing other shows.
  - **C** gained competence through learning from mistakes.
  - **D** felt unsupported by their new colleagues.

2 What point does Eva make about her daily experience in producing the show?
  - **A** she found it exciting to operate in a new environment
  - **B** she exploited other people to meet her own objectives
  - **C** she enjoyed the tense atmosphere around her
  - **D** she appreciated the sense of reward at certain moments

3 Eva feels that the show became popular because of
  - **A** the amount of work that went into its preliminary stages.
  - **B** the appeal it held for people's traditional tastes.
  - **C** the careful timing of its initial launch.
  - **D** the manner in which the audience participated in its filming.

4 How did Eric feel about what he overheard in the studio?
  - **A** disappointed that certain information had not been revealed to him
  - **B** concerned about how the show had been advertised
  - **C** reluctant to discuss his worries with other people
  - **D** surprised that his instincts about the investors had been wrong

5 Eric suggests that their decision to leave the TV show came as a direct result of
  - **A** assessing the applications of unsuitable candidates.
  - **B** evaluating their ability to make successful business decisions.
  - **C** agreeing that the paperwork involved was excessive.
  - **D** collaborating with the investors while filming the show.

6 When asked about setting up their new consultancy, Eva and Eric disagree about
  - **A** the sense of caution they feel about their job security.
  - **B** the lack of thoroughness in their preparation.
  - **C** the advantage they have over their competitors.
  - **D** the importance of learning more about start-up businesses.

SPEAKING PART 2

1 Cross out any phrase (1–6) which does not mean the same as the others and tick (✔) if they are all synonyms.

1 as such / then again / having said that
2 it goes without saying / it's fair to say / it's open to question
3 I'd imagine that / I suspect that / presumably
4 in a way / with respect to / to a certain extent
5 specifically / in particular / specially
6 as for / with regard to / as opposed to

2 18 Look at the photos and listen to a candidate answering a Part 2 exam task. Then complete the extracts with phrases from exercise 1.

1 _____, you could argue that the two couldn't be more different.

2 I think _____ that in the first image, these people are motivated by a desire to connect with nature and, more _____, wildlife…

3 _____, it might just be the latest project that they're assigned to.

4 _____ the problems they might face somewhere like this, _____ that the extreme weather would cause ongoing issues…

5 In the second image, _____ these people are motivated by making money.

6 _____ difficulties, _____ it could feel pretty claustrophobic sometimes…

The director of the company you work for has noticed an especially high number of younger members of staff leaving over the past year, and has asked you for ideas on how to prevent this from happening in future.

Write a proposal suggesting reasons why younger staff members might be unhappy, what could be done to address the situation and explaining how any such changes would benefit the company.

Write your proposal.

1 **The language in bold in these sentences is too informal for this proposal. Read the model text and find and underline the more formal alternatives.**

1 ... and to recommend changes which **should sort out the mess once and for all**.

2 The **main things people are moaning about** can be broken down into three categories:

3 The grey/beige colour scheme **makes everyone totally miserable** (not least during the winter months).

4 **It'll be more pricey, sure**, but the effect on morale would be immediate.

5 ... but the sessions should ultimately aim to **make sure everyone stops having a go at everyone else all the time**.

6 **Make these changes and I reckon that** younger staff should be happier and less likely to leave.

2 **Find three sentences in the model text that do not belong in this proposal.**

3 **In which of the following text types would the three sentences from Exercise 3 be more appropriate?**

> a review   an essay   a report
> a formal letter   an informal email

Reply Forward ✉ 🔍 🏠

<u>Introduction</u>

Dear Mr Coxen,

This proposal is intended to assess the main reasons why the turnover of younger members of staff is currently so high, and to recommend changes which might address the situation most effectively.

<u>Reasons for staff displeasure</u>

The main areas of concern can be broken down into three categories:

• Workplace environment, i.e. the design/decoration within the building
• Lack of career progression – newer recruits feel that there are no opportunities for promotion
• Staff interaction – the 'us and them' culture that exists between younger and older colleagues

<u>Suggestions for Improvement</u>

To take each point in order, I would firstly recommend attending to the office design. Please don't take this the wrong way, I don't want our friendship to suffer, you know that, don't you? The grey/beige colour scheme can have a negative effect on people's moods (not least during the winter months), so at the very least a new paint job is required. However, a more effective idea might be if the office were given a complete makeover by an interior design company. More expensive it might work out, certainly, but the effect on morale would be immediate.

Despite many people feeling stuck in the same post, the company does promote staff regularly and does offer a 'mentor' system for career progression. As such, the main issue is raising awareness of this, so the communications department should be tasked with frequently relaying information about such opportunities.

In terms of the age group split, I would suggest setting up training sessions for both older employees and their younger colleagues to attend together. Not only should this allow everyone to air their grievances, but the sessions should ultimately aim to promote and ensure collaboration and supportiveness. Last year, I was lucky enough to take part in a course called 'Work Wonders', and, without going overboard, I have to say that it took my breath away.

<u>Main Outcome</u>

If these adaptations were made, I firmly believe younger staff should be happier and less likely to leave. Consequently, the company would further benefit financially from the reduction in recruitment costs.

GRAMMAR

1 Correct the mistakes in the underlined parts of the sentences to make correct participle clauses.

1 <u>Having experienced never a flotation tank before</u>, I was astonished at how relaxed it made me feel.

Never having experienced/Having never experienced …

2 When Dr Stanton released the results of her experiments into memory and intelligence, her peers, <u>were expecting a different outcome</u>, were astonished.

3 <u>Giving encouragement rather than criticism</u>, people tend to perform more confidently and obtain better results.

4 I think the course I'm going to apply for is <u>the one offers you</u> your money back if you don't pass.

5 There are so many compelling theories about human behaviour, but research into these ideas will never take place <u>if considered it unethical</u>.

6 A search has begun for the person <u>who believed to have hacked the government's IT system</u>.

7 Having reached the top of the mountain, I sat down, <u>gazed out at the awe-inspiring view</u>.

2 Complete the second sentence in each pair with the correct nouns and prepositions/adverbs so that it means the same as the first. Use words from both boxes and the words in bold in the first sentence to help you.

transformation	growth	recognition
deterioration	explanation	

for	in (x4)	of

1 My aunt has just been given an award **that recognises** her tireless campaigning for improved social care.

My aunt has just been given an award _____ _____ _____ her tireless campaigning for improved social care.

2 Over the past decade, people's attitudes towards mental health issues **have changed** radically.

There has been a radical _____ _____ people's attitudes towards mental health over the past decade.

3 The number of applications for our *Dream Interpretation* course **is growing** which is almost overwhelming.

We are experiencing a sudden _____ _____ the number of applications for our *Dream Interpretation* course which is almost overwhelming.

4 No one can **explain** why his performance at school is **getting worse**.

There is no _____ _____ the _____ _____ his performance at school.

VOCABULARY

1 Correct the spelling of the common adjectives. Tick (✔) any which are spelled correctly.

1 overwelmed ....
2 devestated ....
3 concerned ....
4 apprcitive ....
5 humiliaited ....
6 descouraged ....
7 reluctant ....
8 speechless ....
9 astoneshed ....
10 thrilled ....

2 Complete the sentences with the correct words from Exercise 1. There are three words you do not need.

1 Although my grandfather saved many lives as a fireman, he was a bit of a .... hero and never enjoyed public attention.

2 In the debate today, the government official was .... by his opponents, who defeated all his arguments with a more impressive agenda for progress.

3 Teenagers are prone to making certain choices that put them at risk. But, in such situations, what should .... parents do?

4 Our server crashed today after being .... by demand from people wanting to find out more about our new yoga retreat.

5 Although it was plain for all to see that he was nervous, Billy gave an amazing talk today to a clearly .... audience.

6 For too long we have watched as vast areas of natural beauty around the world have been .... by natural disasters. Collectively, the time to act is now.

7 My parents weren't exactly .... when I told them I wanted to drop out of university and become a yoga instructor.

3 Choose the correct options to complete the advertisement for a mindfulness retreat.

Complete the sentences with idioms with *think/thought* and the words in bold. Use between three and five words for each answer.

1 My dad always used to say, *"don't do, think"*, but I never really paid attention to him. Actually, **COME**, I pretty much ignored all his advice at that time. How naive I was.
come to think of it

2 A spontaneous approach to life is not so much about the ability to **FEET** – it's more to do with being fully prepared for every eventuality before it happens.
....

3 Everyone has been going on about what a great book The Zen Philosophy is, but I didn't **MUCH**, to be honest.
....

4 She is **HIGHLY** by her peers and tutors in the Philosophy department. ....

5 When my friend asked me to go and see a hypnotist with her, I had to **TWICE** before agreeing, but she was right in the end – we had an amazing time.
....

6 I still get anxiety dreams about going into my final exams without a pen and knowing nothing but, **BACK** how stressful that period was, there's clearly a reason that I do.
....

7 I'm so sorry. I completely lost **TRAIN** there. What were we talking about? ....

New Year ... New You?

How did you see in the New Year? Party? Dinner? Perhaps you over-indulged a little with the celebrating and **(1)** *unwinding/gathering/embracing* with friends...

Now you're **(2)** *dreading/envisaging/daydreaming* going back to the office, the classroom, or wherever else it is that you seem to spend far, far too much of your time. Perhaps you've begun seriously **(3)** *reflecting/evaluating/ contemplating* on your life and wondering how to put the brakes on.

Take a moment to **(4)** *gather/grasp/tackle* your thoughts ... and book yourself a weekend away in our dazzling health and relaxation spa, set in the gorgeous Dunbreck countryside. Relax and **(5)** *contemplate/envisage/ daydream* the surroundings in an atmosphere of true serenity, together with like-minded souls seeking solace and support, with whom you can **(6)** *daydream/embrace/contemplate* about a life free from stress.

During your mindfulness classes, you will learn how to meditate, clear your mind and **(7)** *embrace/tackle/envisage* your inner strength. By the time you leave, you will have fully **(8)** *grasped/tackled/gathered* the importance of keeping your thoughts in peak condition, becoming more than able to cope with whatever life throws at you.

For questions 1–8, read the text below and decide which answer (A, B, C or D) best fits each gap. There is an example at the beginning (0).

Example:

0 A seeing   **B** placing   **C** freeing   **D** losing

0 A ☐ B ☐ C ☐ D ■

To flock or not to flock?

Staring up as a flock of birds swarms together, I am conscious of **(0)** .... myself entirely in contemplation. Of course, the displays are aesthetically remarkable, but what strikes me most is that the behaviour **(1)** .... by birds flying in this way says so much about what we, as a species, have lost. Conventional **(2)** .... dictates that we are forever on the march towards progress, but at what cost?

(3) .... human societies once defined themselves by this type of collective mentality, in modern cultures, individuality is **(4)** .... over a common sense of purpose, and the desire to simply look out for one another is becoming lost. We are increasingly at the **(5)** .... of anyone seeking to take advantage of us. Flocking, though, offers **(6)** .... in numbers, since any potential predator is more easily spotted, and is also denied the advantage of quickly being able to **(7)** .... weaker members of the group. It is impossible to **(8)** .... the importance of a philosophy in which we protect each other from the worst the world can throw at us.

1	**A**	presented	**B**	exhibited	**C**	revealed	**D** exposed
2	**A**	wisdom	**B**	insight	**C**	consideration	**D** knowledge
3	**A**	Conversely	**B**	Whereas	**C**	Nonetheless	**D** Despite
4	**A**	ranked	**B**	prioritised	**C**	ordered	**D** selected
5	**A**	power	**B**	mercy	**C**	pity	**D** control
6	**A**	protection	**B**	security	**C**	defence	**D** safety
7	**A**	single out	**B**	set aside	**C**	settle up	**D** square off
8	**A**	overdo	**B**	oversimplify	**C**	overstate	**D** overcome

LISTENING PART 1

19 You will hear three different extracts. For questions 1–6, choose the answer (A, B or C) which fits best according to what you hear. There are two questions for each extract.

Extract One

1 What is the man doing?
- **A** doubting the usefulness of intelligence tests
- **B** complaining about the nature of recruitment processes
- **C** emphasising how information is open to individual interpretation

2 How does the woman feel about intelligence tests?
- **A** puzzled why people do not take them seriously
- **B** critical of the science that is used to support them
- **C** not sure how they will be used in the longer term

Extract Two

3 What point is the man making about the wheel?
- **A** its importance is often underestimated
- **B** its invention required great creativity
- **C** its simplicity is its greatest strength

4 What do they both think about the way inventions are evaluated?
- **A** that people confine themselves to a narrow view of history
- **B** that people tend to make suggestions based on negative impacts
- **C** that people overlook the practical aspects of particular inventions

Extract Three

5 What was the woman's criticism of the way in which the course was delivered?
- **A** it focused excessively on irrelevant themes
- **B** it expected too much of participants
- **C** it diminished a key central aspect

6 Since attending the course, the man has felt
- **A** newly aware of the value of reflection
- **B** more assertive in his daily interactions
- **C** better able to identify with other people

SPEAKING PART 4

1 Read the advice (1–6) about the Speaking Part 4 discussion task and decide if you think it is G (good advice) or B (bad advice).

1 During the discussion, talk as much as possible, even talk over the other candidate if necessary, because, after all, you are competing with them for a better mark.

2 Make sure that your answers to the questions are extended. Justify what you say with explanations, reasons, examples, and so on.

3 Don't admit you don't know how to answer a question or use phrases like 'Let me think' or 'That's a difficult question' to give yourself time to think of a good answer. The examiner will think you are deliberately wasting time.

4 A good strategy for difficult questions is to try and answer the question from more than one perspective.

5 You shouldn't disagree with your partner.

6 You will lose marks if the examiner disagrees with your opinions, so try to avoid this.

2 20 Now listen to a teacher responding to the advice in Exercise 1. Match the responses (A–F) to the advice (1–6).

3 20 Listen again and write the phrases he uses at the start of each response to agree or disagree. Then decide if they are used to A (agree) or D (disagree).

- **A** ....
- **B** ....
- **C** ....
- **D** ....
- **E** ....
- **F** ....

4 21 Listen to this extract from Part 4's questions. Based on the advice in the previous exercises, choose G (the girl) or B (the boy) for the following statements.

1 The candidate rudely interrupts the other candidate.
2 The candidate asks the other candidate questions to involve them in the discussion.
3 The candidate talks for too long when answering one of the questions and goes off the point.
4 The candidate uses a strategy to buy time to answer a difficult question.
5 The candidate answers a question by looking at it from two different viewpoints.

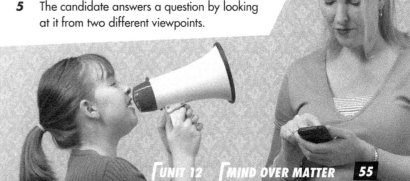

13 LIFESTYLE CHOICES

GRAMMAR

1 Complete the second sentence so that it has a similar meaning to the first sentence, using the word given. Do not change the word given. Use between three and six words.

1 The cabin we bought is not very far at all from the lake.

WALK

From the lake, it's _____ our new cabin.

2 If you enjoyed your stay at the spa, we would love you to leave a review on StayGuide.

APPRECIATE

If you enjoyed your stay at the spa, we would _____ a review on StayGuide.

3 In life, don't just dream about what you want to achieve – get on with it.

GOOD

In life, _____ about what you want to achieve – get on with it.

4 They had no idea if their first business would work when they set it up.

WHETHER

When they set up their first business, there _____ it would work or not.

5 At your age, you absolutely must take responsibility for your lifestyle choices.

QUESTION

At your age, there's _____ responsibility for your lifestyle choices.

6 You have a responsibility to tell your parents now you're thinking about dropping out of college.

OWE

Now you're thinking about dropping out of college, _____ to tell them.

2 Correct the mistakes with pronouns in the sentences.

1 Whenever you go, and whatever busy you are, you will always be able to find inner peace if you know how to meditate.

2 It's always been an ambition of her to give up work and live off the land.

3 There are people from all walks of life who find themself drawn to the adrenaline rush of extreme sports, however the dangers.

4 People worry too much about life's unlikely risks, such as being in an aeroplane crash, and don't pay enough attention to the more likely one, such as being overworked.

5 Home-school educations, such as my brother's and mines, are often viewed with suspicion by those who have come through the conventional system.

6 When you reach a crossroads in life, you must make sure that, whatever route you choose, it is one that makes you happy, even if that does mean taking a chance.

7 Be careful with cheap surfboards as it's a common characteristic of them to split in half if you try and catch a wave that is too big.

8 Who it was that convinced him to change career at the age of fifty, I thank them from the bottom of my heart.

9 Of all the suggestions made for an adventure holiday, Marcia was delighted when it was the hers that everyone liked the most.

10 There are a huge number of good scuba diving schools out there, but let me know if you would like me to recommend ones in particular.

VOCABULARY

1 Complete the conversation with the words in the box.

call double hot jeopardy precaution
plunge reckless chance stake threatened

A: Have you heard about Marco? He's in
   (1) .... water again.

B: Why? What is it this time?

A: Well, you know he's been seeing that Chinese girl
   he met on his language degree? Well, after a
   whirlwind relationship, they decided to take the
   (2) .... and get married.

B: You're joking!

A: I'm not. They decided to do it back in her home
   country, but when her parents met him, they
   decided he wasn't suitable for their daughter. It
   was all called off – the wedding, the relationship,
   everything.

B: Are you serious?

A: Sadly, yes. The thing is, he hadn't taken the
   (3) .... of **(4)** .... –checking his study
   visa, which apparently expired last month. Now
   they won't let him back into the country, so he's
   stuck over there. Even for Marco, it's unbelievable
   that he'd just leave something like that to
   (5) .... So, now his place at university here
   is in **(6)** .... and his parents are so angry
   they've **(7)** .... to disown him.

B: But it's our final year, there's so much at
   (8) ....! How could he be so **(9)** ....?

A: Who knows? Hopefully this will be the wake-up
   (10) .... he needs. But I seriously doubt it.

2 22 Listen and check your answers to
Exercise 1.

3 Choose the correct options to complete the
sentences. Sometimes more than one answer is
possible.

1 We saw some astonishing sights travelling in the
   US. The Grand Canyon was breathtaking, but the
   crowning *moment/glory/achievement* was
   Snoqualmie Falls.

2 Mountain climbing is extremely dangerous, so I'd advise you
   to treat it with the utmost *caution/discretion/respect*.

3 Against overwhelming *support/odds/victory*, Sara recovered
   from her injury in time to compete in the skiing championships.

4 Swimming with dolphins has always been a burning *ambition/
   desire/issue* of mine.

5 My parents force me to take piano lessons in the vain *effort/
   hope/attempt* that I might want to become a musician.

6 It doesn't take long to become a more confident scuba diver,
   but don't be lulled into a false *hope/start/sense* of security.
   Even the most experienced divers put safety first.

PUSH YOURSELF /C2

1 Tick the correct expressions with *time*.
Then correct the remaining expressions.

1 grab him at a bad time   *catch him at a bad time*
2 in front of her time
3 after biding their time
4 had my hands on time
5 it's only a matter of time
6 behind the times
7 had a time of my life
8 race against timing
9 in the nick of time
10 time will say

2 Complete the sentences with the correct forms of
the expressions from Exercise 1.

1 We suddenly realised we had got carried away
   while exploring the rainforest, and it was a
   .... to make it
   back to the boat before the sun set.

2 One day, out of the blue, I decided to try and
   conquer my vertigo by bungee jumping. Terrified
   though I was, I ....
   and went straight back up to do it again.

3 My great-grandmother was very much
   .... When she
   was eighteen, she decided she wasn't going to get
   married until she was at least thirty, and only after
   she had travelled and seen the world.

4 At the point when I was seriously considering setting
   up my own surfing academy, I was suddenly made
   redundant. It was perfect timing. Suddenly I
   ...., which is vital
   if you're going to follow your dream.

5 After we sold the car and most of what we owned,
   we left our jobs and bought a houseboat. Only
   .... whether we
   made the right decision, but we're feeling positive
   for now.

6 If you really want your dad to let you take a gap
   year, try not to ....
   when you ask. I reckon you'll only get one chance
   for him to agree.

23 **You will hear a blogger called David Jensen giving a talk about risk-taking photographers on social media. For questions 1–8, complete the sentences with a word or short phrase.**

EXTREME-SELFIE HUNTERS

David explains how extreme selfie-hunters, in search of a
(1) _____*perfect shot*_____ , frequently engage in risky behaviour.

David uses the word **(2)** _____ to describe the popular
status of extreme-selfie photography.

When talking about the picture taken from the top of the building, David states it was the
(3) _____ of the photographer that most impressed him.

David explains that people used online **(4)** _____
services to ensure that their pictures could be seen worldwide.

David acknowledges the importance of the **(5)** _____
shown to famous selfie-hunters by their fans.

David says that there was a shift in approach to this art form as the
(6) _____ of its new contributors became more
prominent.

David believes that the **(7)** _____ of extreme-selfie
photography is often ignored by its critics.

David thinks the available **(8)** _____ confirm that people
rarely put themselves in danger through a desire to copy others.

WRITING PART 2: LETTER/EMAIL

1 Which two of the following phrase pairs is correct for the beginning and ending of a formal letter/email?

1	Dear Sir/Madam,	→ Thanks for reading,
2	Hey,	→ Ciao!
3	Dear Editor,	→ Yours faithfully,
4	Dear Sue,	→ Yours faithfully,
5	Dear Ms Collins,	→ Yours sincerely,
6	To whom it may concern,	→ Best wishes,

2 Read the email below and find synonyms for the words (1–8) in the paragraphs shown.

1 claims .... **(A)**
2 choose .... **(A)**
3 affects .... **(A)**
4 selfishly .... **(B)**
5 taking part .... **(B)**
6 a period of work experience .... **(B)**
7 harmful .... **(C)**
8 point of view .... **(C)**

> A lifestyle website has published an article which argues that taking a gap year* is damaging to a young person's development and career prospects. You have read the article and think that its ideas are too negative. Write a letter to the website editor in which you explain your reasons for disagreeing with the article, giving your opinion on the value of taking a gap year.
>
> *a year off between finishing school education and going to university or starting a job, often used for travelling
>
> Write your <u>email</u>. You do not need to include email addresses.

3 Choose adjectives and adverbs from the box to complete the email. Use each option only once.

> frankly   serious   enormous
> incredibly   wide   ~~invariably~~
> negatively   real   various   traditional

● ● ● ◀ ▢

Reply Forward ✉

Dear Editor,

(A) I am writing in response to Jamie Solo's article published on your website last week, in which he asserts that, should a young person opt to take a gap year, their growth as a person **(1)** *invariably* suffers, and that doing so **(2)** .... impacts their future employment ambitions.

(B) Firstly, I would like to pick up on the claim that year-long breaks from education are taken for one reason: to travel the world, self-interestedly avoiding responsibility. In no way is this the case for the majority, and I would argue that this is an **(3)** .... stereotypical view. The fact of the matter is, travelling is just one of the **(4)** .... options available, and young people do use their time wisely, engaging in a range of activities, such as taking an internship or a course, or simply reflecting on the route they want to follow next in life.

(C) The second point I would like to pick up on is the idea that a gap year is detrimental to a person's career further down the line. **(5)** ...., I believe this to be an outdated perspective. In today's world, employers are looking for well-rounded individuals who can bring a **(6)** .... range of skills and perspectives to their position. The **(7)** .... career path of 'school, university, job' no longer needs to be followed by everyone.

(D) As a final comment, I would like to emphasise the **(8)** .... value I see in stepping back from education for a short time. Not only do young people experience a **(9)** .... sense of progression in their ability to make choices, but also their awareness of social contexts outside of school or college develops. At the same time, their preparation for the demands of university-level study is given a **(10)** .... boost.

Yours faithfully,

14 LOOKING AFTER YOURSELF

GRAMMAR

1 Complete the second sentence so that it has a similar meaning to the first sentence, using the word given. Do not change the word given. Use between three and six words.

1 I have to get twelve hours' rest each day, as instructed by my doctor.

REQUIRE

My doctor's _____ get twelve hours' rest each day.

2 Up until 1950, doctors would reassure people about the positive physical effects that smoking had.

SUPPOSED

Up until 1950, smoking _____ positive physical effects.

3 We need to revise our menu thoroughly to attract more customers.

THOROUGH

To attract more customers, there needs _____ our menu.

4 I was wondering if you could please tell me where the nearest health food shop is.

KIND

Would you _____ tell me where the nearest health food shop is?

5 Over the next month, I plan to reduce my calorie intake by a third.

INTENTION

Over the next month, my _____ my calorie intake by a third.

6 You won't feel in good shape until you get enough exercise.

MORE

Only _____ you begin to feel in good shape.

7 I have never visited a health spa before but I would love to go to one.

DESPITE

Despite _____ before, I would love to go to a health spa.

8 Chris only managed to complete the marathon because he'd trained so intensely.

FOR

If it _____ training, Chris would never have completed the marathon.

2 Complete the text below with the word that best fits each gap.

Is your doctor
who they say they are?

While some people are content simply to be a patient in the surgery room, others are less **(1)** _____ . There has been an alarming rise over the past decade in the number of people posing **(2)** _____ GPs. These are people with **(3)** _____ or no knowledge of how the human body even works, yet they somehow manage to get **(4)** _____ officially registered, and set up as certified medical practitioners. These people will often have developed a sophisticated, sympathetic questioning technique, much of **(5)** _____ is designed to put the patient's mind **(6)** _____ ease. At the same time, they can only perform one or two basic procedures, so it is clear to see where the dangers lie. In the past year, government legislation has set clearer punishments for imitating a doctor, but this really **(7)** _____ to have been the case from the very beginning.

3 Correct the two mistakes in each sentence.

1 I did applied to join that exclusive fitness club, but I never heard from them back.

2 As unreliable that he is, he has promised to me to take me to the game.

3 The tennis club was opened by local hero Tim Mensch is arguably best-equipped in the city.

4 Hadn't my dad spent most of his life eating rubbish, he wouldn't have been so overweight now.

5 I was delighted to been invited to speak at the weight-loss conference – opportunities as this don't come up very often.

6 It's time for few changes in attitude. Hopefully, the whole world will soon choose going vegetarian.

7 The canteen here is awful. Bring your own lunch to work is the only way to guaranteed of a nutritious meal.

VOCABULARY

1 Correct the underlined word form mistakes in the sentences.

1 I hear Daniel is still ill. How long has it been since he first started feeling <u>poor</u>?

2 It's such a shame that my favourite food has so little <u>nutritious</u> value – but you just can't beat hot dogs, can you?

3 A woman is suing her local hospital after her recent <u>surgeon</u> was administered without proper anaesthetic.

4 The ackee fruit is delicious when eaten ripe, but <u>poisoned</u> if it is consumed while still yellow.

5 In a recent survey of chefs regarding the <u>allergies</u> that they hesitate to cook with, peanuts topped the list.

6 A man was taken to hospital today in a <u>life-threatened</u> condition after being hit by an ambulance.

2 Match the sentence halves, changing the words in bold to the synonyms so that they form correct collocations.

1 Most medical professionals believe there is little hard **proof** for homeopathy providing any sort *evidence (B)*

2 After the funding scandal had come to light, there was the inevitable **firing**

3 I'm surprised my grandmother is still alive after such a long **past**

4 Prolonged smoking of cigarettes will most likely cause a **lowering**

5 A wide variety of conditions could cause your **absence**

6 *Nitey* insomnia medication has been found to cause the embarrassing **additional**-effect

A of illness – she's ninety-four!

B of cure for illness.

C of appetite, such as feeling over-anxious or stressed.

D of breath and other health complications.

E of occasionally falling asleep in public.

F of the hospital director.

3 Complete the words to answer the questions. The first letters are given to help you.

1 What do you sometimes get when you have a cold?
A **r** _____ **n** _____

2 What can make it difficult to swallow?
A **s** _____ **t** _____

3 What rises if you eat too much salt or take too little exercise?
b _____ **p** _____

4 What do you need to eat to stay healthy?
A **b** _____ **d** _____

5 What do long-haul flights interfere with?
Your **b** _____ **c** _____

PUSH YOURSELF C2

1 Complete the health idioms with the words in the box using the definitions in brackets.

alive	bitter	death's	kicking	door	medicine
mend	pill	swallow	take	taste	turn	under
weather	worse				

1 _____ the _____ **(feeling poorly)**

2 _____ a _____ for the _____ **(become more unwell)**

3 at _____ _____ **(extremely ill)**

4 _____ and _____ **(fit and healthy)**

5 a _____ to _____ **(difficult to accept)**

6 on the _____ **(getting better)**

7 a _____ of your own _____ **(bad treatment being returned to you)**

You are going to read an extract from a magazine article about Generation Z. Six paragraphs have been removed from the extract. Choose from the paragraphs A–G the one which fits each gap (1–6). There is one extra paragraph which you do not need to use.

Health Wise

65-year-old blogger Ian Bradfield investigates the physical and mental health obsessions of Generation Z (people born between the mid-1990s and approximately 2010).

While many people of my age care increasingly little about their fading levels of fitness, a health scare five years ago shocked me into action. I made dramatic changes to every aspect of my existence: food intake, exercise routines and lifestyle choices. In my eyes, I soon became – in health terms, at least – the equal of anyone a third of my age.

1

I pay a visit to my granddaughter, Alicia, born in 1995, and a proud member of 'Gen Z'. Like so many of her age today, despite ever-present worries about job security, she has set up her own business. While we discuss her life and career often, I have never yet visited the studio where she works as a personal dietician, trainer and lifestyle coach, advising clients how to embrace every aspect of modern well-being.

2

This is ably demonstrated by Alicia as she shows me round her studio, packed with all manner of technology and gadgets. I wouldn't know where to start. We run through a mock consultation, in which I play the part of her potential client. I am struck by the way she seems to side-step direct questioning of my physical and mental health. 'That's the impression people get,' she tells me, 'but the reality is, I am constantly trying to isolate aspects of their personality to build the bigger picture'.

3

It makes complete sense, the more I think about it, to approach life in this way. Before long, proof of these principles arrives in the shape of a client, and Alicia introduces me to Emily. She is the very picture of health: glowing skin, shining teeth, an aura of calmness around her. What's more, she is demonstrably pleased to share her diet, workout and meditation tips with an old-timer like me.

4

Statistically-speaking, Gen Z-ers – when taken together, that is – are three times as likely to be obese than people of my generation were at the same age. Despite combining all that state-of-the-art training equipment with instant online access to thousands of superfood recipes, research suggests that they are actually more out of shape than I used to be at the same stage of life. I ask Alicia an interesting question. Does their rejection of risky lifestyle choices from the past, such as smoking, therefore count for nothing?

5

The fact is, one addiction can so easily be replaced by another. Sure, our smartphones are packed with wonderful apps that monitor our heart rates or suggest new superfoods, but today's dependency on modern technology has led to a lot more time spent sitting down. Leisure, social and work activities are excessively conducted while slouched in front of screens, and often all are done at the same time.

6

As I leave her studio, I feel energised. During my journey home, I reflect on what I have learnt today, and come to a decision. Shortly after I walk through my front door, I check my diary, call Alicia and book my second consultation.

A So, keeping things separate is important. Paradoxically, while a holistic approach in which the inter-connectedness of all elements of well-being is emphasised here, each must be addressed individually for any effect to be felt.

B 'It's a balancing act,' she explains. Though these self-destructive habits of a few decades ago are a thing of the past, 'don't kid yourself that you're in the clear, simply because you keep a food diary or sign up to every gym class you can'.

C That said, the evidence of my own eyes tells me that, for every young adult slumped in a pile on the sofa playing video games, there are dozens more who watch over mind, body and soul. Look no further than my granddaughter.

D The search for a perfect state of health and well-being has become increasingly prominent over the past decade, and the world is better off as a result. The one criticism I have is exactly that insistence on posting everything online.

E At least, that was what I initially thought. But the fact is that, when it comes to obsessing over daily protein consumption, or how many steps you have taken since waking up, Generation Z puts all my efforts entirely in the shade.

F In front of me, then, is evidence of the benefits that a clean lifestyle can bring. Surely, this alone demonstrates how their generation has uncovered the secrets of health and happiness? Current studies suggest otherwise.

G Livelihoods such as these are alien to people like me, but they are common today; the concept of 'multi-tasking' is not so much a skill that has to be acquired (as in my case), but rather an obligatory aspect of life, practically innate from birth.

You see the following announcement on a healthy eating website, *Tried and Tasted*.

Send us a review of a restaurant you have visited which serves healthy food.

Tell us how much you enjoyed your experience, what you remember most about it, and whether or not you would recommend this place to our readers.

Write your review.

1 Read the review and choose the best title (A–C).

A The benefits of veganism
B Review of *Legume with a View*
C Eating Out … of my Comfort Zone

Home
About
Reviews
Search

Staring at the menu, trying to decide what I fancied, reality suddenly hit me … not one dish contained meat. Sure, every dish on there was nicely described, but would I be able to enjoy a meal made ¹<u>only of vegetables</u>? More to the point, would I even feel full at the end?

The answer is a resounding 'yes'. *Legume with a View* is ²<u>an excellent restaurant</u>, from its picturesque location overlooking the river, to its knowledgeable and well-trained staff, and ³<u>its delicious food</u>. Had I known that my eyes would be opened to such a world of new tastes, I would have visited vegan restaurants long before now. Each of the five courses I ordered was skilfully cooked and looked ⁴<u>really beautiful</u> on the plate – a picture-perfect example of healthy eating.

⁵<u>My favourite dish was</u> the aubergine with miso and cabbage, which was ⁶<u>impossible to forget</u>. If there was one dish I could eat every day of my life, this may well be it. That is not to say that the other courses were lacking in any way – ⁷<u>they really weren't</u>. As I stared out of the window at the river, with the delightful waiting staff on hand to cater to any of my requests, I almost entirely forgot about having a conversation with my dinner companion.

I was ⁸<u>surprised and very happy</u> that my concerns about not having enough to eat had been so misguided, we paid the bill and said goodbye. ⁹<u>I haven't often</u> left a restaurant as full and content as I was that evening.

Final sentence: ....

2 Replace the underlined sections of the review (1–9) with the phrases in the box to make it more emphatic and persuasive.

an absolute winner   astonished and delighted   rarely have I
bland they most certainly were not   its mind-blowing dishes
nothing short of gorgeous   of vegetables and vegetables alone
a special mention must go to   utterly unforgettable

3 Choose the best conclusion for the review (A–C). Give reasons for your choice.

A Overall, I would recommend this restaurant to anyone because, as discussed above, the food, views and service were excellent. I remember everything about it very clearly.

B I would not hesitate to recommend this restaurant to readers of *Tried and Tasted,* but I do have one request in return – please, take me with you when you go.

C This is definitely a restaurant I would recommend to *Tried and Tasted* readers, although I did forget to mention that it is actually quite expensive. Thus, maybe they should bring the prices down a little.

ACKNOWLEDGEMENTS

The authors and publishers acknowledge the following sources of copyright material and are grateful for the permissions granted. While every effort has been made, it has not always been possible to identify the sources of all the material used, or to trace all copyright holders. If any omissions are brought to our notice, we will be happy to include the appropriate acknowledgements on reprinting and in the next update to the digital edition, as applicable.

Key: S = Starter, U = Unit.

Photography
All the photographs are sourced from Getty Images.

S: Westend61; Skynesher/E+; Image by Catherine MacBride/Moment; Sengchyeteo/Moment; **U1:** Klaus Vedfelt/DigitalVision; Ferrantraite/E+; Pixelfit/E+; **U2:** Bim/E+; PeopleImages/E+; JordanSiemens/DigitalVision; Kiszon Pascal/Moment; **U3:** PM Images/DigitalVision; Matthew Leete/DigitalVision; Westend61; NIKLAS HALLE'N/AFP; **U4:** April30/E+; Science Photo Library - ANDRZEJ WOJCICKI/Brand X Pictures; Cjp/E+; Michael Roberts/Moment; **U5:** Phil Boorman/Cultura; Photographer is my life/Moment; Mixetto/E+; Miguel Sanz/Moment; **U6:** Urbazon/iStock/Getty Images Plus; Nikada/E+; J.Castro/Moment; South_agency/iStock/Getty Images Plus; Chris Whitehead/Cultura; Xavierarnau/Cultura; **U7:** Red Chopsticks; Cristian Negroni/500px; Pixelfit/E+; Olaser/E+; **U8:** AntonioGuillem/iStock/Getty Images Plus; hocus-focus/E+; CASEZY/iStock/Getty Images Plus; Daviles/iStock/Getty Images Plus; Tetra Images/Brand X Pictures; **U9:** Tetra Images/Brand X Pictures; Michael S/500px; Marc Guitard/Moment; Praetorianphoto/E+; **U10:** Image Source/DigitalVision; Matt Lincoln/Cultura; Vincent Laforet/Getty Images Sport; **U11:** 10'000 Hours/DigitalVision; Sturti/E+; Alasdair Turner; Maximilian Stock Ltd/The Image Bank/Getty Images Plus; SolStock/E+; Zero Creatives/Cultura; **U12:** Maskot; Compassionate Eye Foundation/Stone; Sharon Jones-Williams/Moment Open; JGI/Jamie Grill; **U13:** Peepo/E+; Mark C Stevens/Moment; Rodrigo Friscione/Image Source; Peter Muller/Cultura; **U14:** Westend61; PeopleImages/E+; Ada Summer/Stockbyte.

Front cover photography by Supawat Punnanon/EyeEm/Getty Images; Patrick Foto/Getty Images; fStop Images-Caspar Benson/Getty Images; art2002/iStock/Getty Images Plus; Onfokus/E+/Getty Images; primeimages/E+/Getty Images.

Audio produced by Leon Chambers